P9-DNI-320

100 ENGLISH ROSES
for the
AMERICAN GARDEN

SMITH & HAWKEN

100 ENGLISH ROSES *for the* AMERICAN GARDEN

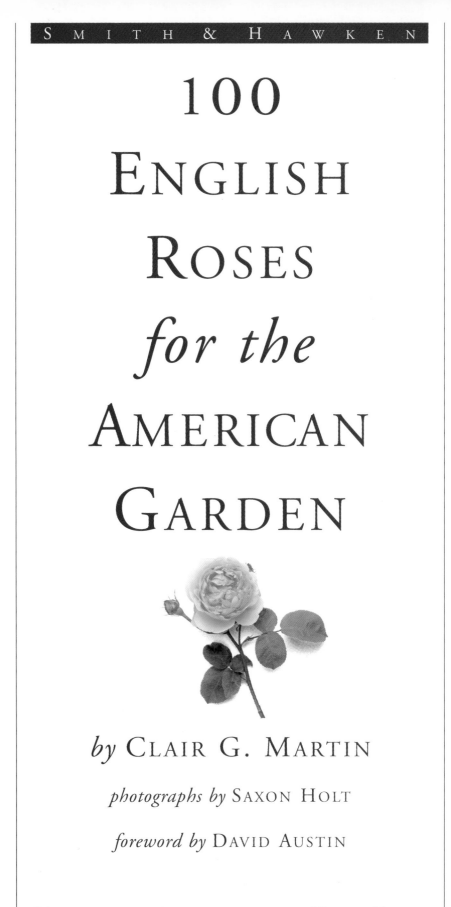

by CLAIR G. MARTIN

photographs by SAXON HOLT

foreword by DAVID AUSTIN

WORKMAN PUBLISHING · NEW YORK

TEXT COPYRIGHT © 1997 BY SMITH & HAWKEN

PHOTOGRAPHY COPYRIGHT © 1997 BY SAXON HOLT

ALL RIGHTS RESERVED. NO PORTION OF THIS BOOK MAY BE REPRODUCED—

MECHANICALLY, ELECTRONICALLY, OR BY ANY OTHER MEANS, INCLUDING

PHOTOCOPYING—WITHOUT WRITTEN PERMISSION OF THE PUBLISHER.

PUBLISHED SIMULTANEOUSLY IN CANADA BY THOMAS ALLEN & SON LIMITED.

LIBRARY OF CONGRESS CATALOGING-IN-PUBLICATION DATA

MARTIN, CLAIR G.

SMITH & HAWKEN 100 ENGLISH ROSES FOR THE AMERICAN GARDEN

BY CLAIR G. MARTIN

PHOTOGRAPHY BY SAXON HOLT

P.   CM.

INCLUDES INDEX

ISBN 0-7611-0185-3

1. ENGLISH ROSES. I. HOLT, SAXON.

II. SMITH & HAWKEN. III. TITLE.

SB411.65.E53M37   1997

635.9'33734--dc21   97-71   CIP

WORKMAN PUBLISHING COMPANY, INC.

708 BROADWAY

NEW YORK, NY 10003-9555

MANUFACTURED IN CHINA

FIRST PRINTING APRIL 1997

10 9 8 7 6 5 4 3 2

CONTENTS

APPENDIXES

Foreword

Every rose behaves a little differently, depending on where it grows. It varies according to soil and climate, the time of flowering, and the nature of the individual season, but most of all according to the country where it is cultivated. This is just one of the things that make roses so intriguing. And for this reason, it is very useful to have a book on English Roses written exclusively for the United States.

I have been agreeably surprised at how well-adapted the English Roses are to climates warmer than that of Britain, in spite of the fact that they were bred for the cool climate of their country of origin. Some of the best English Roses I have seen have been in the U.S.A., Australia, and New Zealand. Given suitable treatment, English Roses tend, on the whole, to grow more strongly in warmer climates—or at least in climates that have warm summers—than they do in a northern European climate, although this is not true of all varieties.

Clair Martin was one of the very first people in the United States to take an interest in English Roses and did much to popularize them in the early days. He obviously appreciates that we are trying to breed into our roses something of the charm, beauty, and fragrance of the Old Roses and, where possible, to improve on this. I have never had the pleasure of meeting Clair, but have often been in contact through the post and on the telephone. I understand that the rose gardens at The Huntington, where he is Curator of Rose Collections, are very beautiful; certainly, he has always struck me as being very knowledgeable and enthusiastic on all matters to do with roses.

This book is superb. I am particularly impressed by the descriptions of individual varieties; they are so full and so acute in their observations. Clair has imbued the book with his passion for English Roses and his appreciation of their place in the American garden.

—DAVID AUSTIN
January 1997

A SHORT HISTORY: "ROSE IS *a* ROSE"

The roses we grow and love today are descended from a long line of garden roses reaching back through many cultures. Roses figured prominently in Roman and Greek festivals; Egyptians placed wreaths of roses in the tombs of their dead; and roses are mentioned on clay tablets written in cuneiform characters by ancient Babylonians. The Chinese also have a rich garden rose tradition extending back to their distant past. Interestingly, Chinese and European rose lines developed along quite independent courses until the beginning of the nineteenth century, when European explorers, botanists, and plant hunters returned from voyages to Asia with living plants and seeds of Chinese Roses.

The repeat-blooming roses we cherish today have existed for little more than a century. Before that time, all the roses grown in the West flowered only once a year, in spring. These once-blooming roses were the flowers known to the Greeks and Romans; they grew in cloistered Medieval gardens; and they were illustrated by Flemish and Italian painters of the Renaissance. Except for one Roman rose, 'Autumn Damask,' all European Roses grown prior to the introduction of the Chinese specimens bloomed just once a year.

Because the Old European Roses were native to Northern Europe, they were impervious to cold and required little care beyond pruning. For the most part, they also possessed a strong, heady fragrance. Blossom color ranged from pure white to mauve, from deep pink to red-purple. Both true crimson red and yellow were unknown

'**P**rospero' *(left foreground) and 'Wenlock' (right foreground) blend into a garden setting, creating a delightful border of perfumed, old-fashioned flowers.*

at that time, and flower form tended to be single, cupped, or flat.

All descriptions of what constitutes an Old Garden Rose (OGR) cite time as the principal defining factor. The most widely accepted interpretation uses the introduction of the first Hybrid Tea, 'La France,' to differentiate between Old and Modern Roses. This particular demarcation, applied by the American Rose Society (ARS) in sanctioned rose shows, recognizes classes of roses introduced before 1867 to be OGRs (Gallica, Damask, Alba, Moss, Centifolia, Tea, China, Portland, Noisette, and Hybrid Perpetual), and Hybrid Teas and classes introduced after 1867 to be Modern Roses (Floribunda, Grandiflora, and Shrub—which includes English Roses). The ARS further sanctions the awarding of a Dowager Queen Award to pre-

1867 roses and a Victorian Queen Award to any rose of a class developed before but introduced after 1867, a time frame obviously significant for many of the world's master rosarians.

A far more practical demarcation would be to use the beginning of the twentieth century as the line between Old Roses and Modern Roses. For the purposes of this book, we will consider any rose introduced before 1901 to be an Old Rose. We are fast approaching the next century, and using this classification will acknowledge the particular "modernness" of the roses of the twentieth century.

OLD GARDEN ROSE CLASSES

We cherish and cultivate Old Roses not only for the sake of growing something old-fashioned, or something that brings a flood of happy childhood memories, but because they help us see where the "rose" has been and where it will be going.

Gardeners have grouped Old European Roses into five classes, distinguishing them by growth habit, prickles, foliage, and flower form. Some of these classes, such as the Gallica and Damask Roses, are truly ancient; others, such as the Centifolia and Moss Roses, just predate the introduction of roses from Asia.

GALLICA ROSES, also known as French or Provence Roses, are the oldest of all garden roses, having been cultivated at least since classical Greek and Roman times. Recognized for their cold-hardiness, Gallicas are once-blooming, compact, low-growing shrubs; stems are covered with needlelike prickles, and the tough, textured foliage is generally a deep matte green, paler on the leaf's underside. Flowers are very full, forming neat, rosette-shaped, strongly fragrant blooms ranging in rich shades of purple, violet, pink, and white, often marked with stripes and splotches of contrasting colors. When grown on their own roots, Gallicas will sucker profusely, forming a dense clump of canes that can spread out across the garden. As noted, Gallica Roses are extremely cold-hardy and can be difficult to get to bloom in the milder zones of the United States. Examples: 'Apothecary's Rose' (from the twelfth century), also known as *Rosa gallica officinalis* and the Red Rose of Lancaster, is one of the most ancient Gallicas still grown today; it has deep pink to light red, semi-double, fragrant flowers. 'Rosa

Mundi' (twelfth century), also known as *R. gallica versicolor,* is a sport (spontaneous mutation) of 'Apothecary's Rose' in which the deep pink, fragrant, semi-double flowers are striped and splashed with white and pink; it blooms better in warmer climates than its parent. 'Cardinal de Richelieu' (1840) has velvety double flowers of smoky purple on a thornless bush growing to 5 feet or so.

DAMASK ROSES trace their origin from remote times along a track nearly parallel to that of the Gallicas. Thought to have been widely cultivated in Persia, the first Damasks to reach Europe were probably brought by Crusaders returning from the Holy Land. The thorny, arching canes and long leaves produce an open, elegant shrub. Known widely for their powerful sweet fragrance, Damasks generally are divided into the once-flowering Summer Damasks and

*G*raced with lovely quartered blooms, 'Abraham Darby' can be grown as a climber or a freestanding shrub.

the Autumn Damasks, which offer a modest repeat-bloom in the fall. Examples: 'Autumn Damask' (ancient), also known as R. damascena bifera, Quatre Saisons, and the Rose of Paestum, is cherished for its wonderful "Damask" fragrance; pale pink, loosely petaled flowers bloom wonderfully in spring and often provide an intermittent bloom throughout the season. 'Mme. Hardy' (1832) bears heart-melting, virginal white, double blooms that display a green button eye; it is powerfully fragrant, with just an additional hint of lemon. 'La Ville de Bruxelles' (1849) produces large, pure pink, quartered, extremely fragrant blossoms on a large, spreading plant.

ALBA ROSES are closely related to *Rosa canina,* the Dog Rose, so named because it was thought that ingesting a concoction made from the hips would cure rabies. Albas are most likely the progeny of natural crosses between the Dog Rose and Damask parents. Europeans grew Albas in ancient times for use in perfume and medicine. Notably quite tolerant of partial shade, Albas are once-bloomers; their blossoms of white or pale pink offer a sweet, heady fragrance, and the gray-green foliage is produced on tall canes covered with prickles. Examples: 'Alba Semi-plena' (ancient) has clustered, single (five-petaled), fragrant white flowers on a 6-foot bush. 'Great Maiden's Blush' (prior to the fifteenth century), also known as Cuisse de Nymphe and La Séduisante, produces seductive blush pink, semi-double, fragrant flowers on a 5-foot plant. 'Félicité Parmentier' (1834)

DOUBLE TROUBLE

All the roses that have ever existed are descended from Wild, or Species, Roses; these display an elemental flower form of just five petals, called single flowers. Increasing the base number of petals comes at the expense of stamen production (the pollen-bearing, or male, part of the flower). In some extreme cases, so many stamens have mutated into petals as to render the flower completely unable to produce viable pollen, making that entire rose naturally infertile. Fertility is so diminished that there is little chance any double-flowered mutations will survive in the wild. Only when they have been collected and saved by gardeners have double-flowered mutations been preserved and passed on from garden to garden.

yields fragrant, double pale pink flowers on canes to 4 feet.

CENTIFOLIA ROSES (literally, "100 petals") probably originated from a chance cross between an Autumn Damask and an Alba. They were the focus of much work by Dutch and French horticulturists during the 1600s. Also known as Cabbage Roses in Europe for their cabbagelike, deeply globular blooms, Centifolias are once-bloomers that produce richly scented, intensely petaled flowers on nodding stems. The brown canes are very thorny and lax to the point of being floppy. The leaves, of the palest green, are rounded and soft. Examples: 'Petite de Hollande' (prior to 1800) forms pale pink, quartered, fragrant miniature flowers on a 3-foot plant. 'Village Maid' (1829) grows to 6 feet with double, globular, richly fragrant white blooms, striped purplish pink. 'Tour de Malakoff' (1856) yields a unique blend of fragrant magenta-purple and violet blooms aging to lavender and gray on a 6-foot shrub.

MOSS ROSES derive their name from the mosslike growth that covers the stems and buds. This mossy growth can vary in color from green to brown, and in texture from soft feathers to stiff prickles. Many also have ornamental, featherlike sepals surrounding the bud. They are beloved for the fragrant oil that lingers on the fingertips when the bloom or bud is touched. Most Moss Roses are once-flowering and are sports from Centifolia and Damask Roses. Examples:

'Crested Moss' (1827), *R. centifolia cristata,* also known as Chapeau de Napoléon, grows to 5 feet with fragrant, double pink flowers and sepals decorated with soft green moss. 'Comtesse de Murinais' (1843) has double, flat, blush pink flowers on a plant of 6 feet. 'Alfred de Dalmas' (1855), also known as Mousseline, bears cupped, loosely petaled, pale pink, sweetly fragrant flowers with decent repeat-bloom on a bush of 3 feet.

REMONTANT OLD GARDEN ROSE CLASSES

Dates differ, but sometime around the end of the eighteenth century or beginning of the nineteenth century, new types of roses began to filter into Europe from Asia. Now recognized as revolutionary, at the time of their introduction they were hardly noticed by gardeners of the

*N*amed for David Austin's mother, the huge peony-like flowers of 'Lilian Austin' are set atop a low-growing, spreading shrub.

*A*lthough not an English Rose, the Hybrid Musk 'Lavender Lassie' would create a
lovely harmony if mixed with low hedges of English Roses.

day. They were what we today classify as China and Tea Roses. Chinas
and Teas brought along three key
traits: remontancy (repeat-bloom),
true deep crimson red flowers, and
the first repeat-blooming Climbing
Roses. One reason the Asian Roses
did not make a larger splash in the
European garden world was that
they were thought to be too cold-
tender to grow outdoors in northern climates. Europeans knew only
that these roses were from hot trop-
ical zones and so treated the first
China and Tea Roses as greenhouse
plants, until it was discovered that
they could be grown outdoors in
the milder zones of England and
France.

It didn't take nurserymen long to
start growing roses produced from
the seed of crosses between Old

European Roses and China and Tea
Roses. At first, because of some
genetic differences between these
groups, all the hybrids produced
were not reblooming, as everyone
had hoped; they were also sterile
and so could not be used to produce
new hybrids. It wasn't until the
1840s that any new hybrid roses
became fertile and repeat-blooming, and then only a few did so.
This came about through the spontaneous mutated doubling of their
chromosomes, which enabled these
hybrids not only to reproduce but
also to pass on the key characteristic of remontancy.

The earliest remontant classes
produced from hybridizing Old
European, China, and Tea Roses
are now also classed as Old Garden
Roses. These remontant Old

Garden Roses were introduced before 1867 and are known as Portlands, Bourbons, Noisettes, and Hybrid Perpetuals.

Heretofore in the Western world, the peak rose garden season was a spring-only event. After the introduction of the China Roses and their ensuing mixed progeny, the rose garden began to celebrate an almost year-round cycle of bloom. Modern Rose lovers tend to overlook the fact that the continuous-blooming roses in our gardens today were not always around in this form.

CHINA ROSES had been cultivated in their homeland for centuries before any were brought to Europe around 1800. Of particular interest to rosarians of the time was their ability to rebloom throughout the summer, a trait not shared by the earlier, European-derived rose classes. Chinas are more delicate in growth than the European Roses in that their slim canes and light green foliage combine to form a dense, twiggy shrub. In addition, many China Roses "suntan": Starting out pale, the flowers actually turn darker in the sun—a stark contrast to most roses, whose colors fade as they age. Best suited for temperate climates, Chinas produce a continuous series of lightly scented blooms throughout the growing season. Modern miniature roses trace their ancestry back to a dwarf China known as 'Rouletti.' All modern, repeat-blooming red roses are direct descendants of one of the original China Roses, 'Slater's Crimson China.' Examples: 'Old Blush' (prior to 1800), also known as Parson's Pink China, yields repeating, clustered pink blooms on a 3-foot plant. 'Mutabilis' (prior to 1900) has single yellow blooms that suntan to orange and red, then finally to crimson on a bush 5 to 6 feet tall. 'Comtesse du Cayla' (1902) bears semi-double, Tea-scented nasturtium-red-tinted-orange flowers on a 3-foot bush.

TEA ROSES probably originated long ago in China as wild crosses between the species *R. gigantea* and a garden form of China Rose. Originally called Tea-Scented China Roses when introduced in Europe, the true origin of the name is obscure. Some think it is derived from a perceived similarity of the scent to the fragrance of fresh tea leaves. Others suggest it stems from the tea chests in which the plants were imported from Asia to Europe. Tea Roses grow as modest shrubs and climbers whose stature is a bit more substantial than that of the Chinas. Widely cherished for their pointed buds that open to nod-

'*Constance Spry*' paints a sensuous fragrant backdrop for a secluded country garden bench.

ding but elegant blooms of pink, cream, apricot, and yellow, these tender plants were highly prized specimens in the Victorian greenhouse. Well-suited for the temperate climates of the United States, Tea Roses were widely grown as far north as Philadelphia at the turn of the century. Examples: 'Duchesse de Brabant' (1857) produces cupped, fragrant pink blossoms on a plant of about 3 feet. 'Lady Hillingdon' (1910) has fragrant, semi-double yellow to apricot blooms on a 5-foot rose. 'Maman Cochet' (1893), 4 feet tall, bears cupped flowers in a blend of lemon, pink, and lavender.

PORTLAND ROSES became popular after 1800 largely because of their ability to bloom repeatedly, a rather rare trait in Old European Roses. Valued for their strong "Old Rose fragrance," the short-stemmed blooms appear to sit directly atop the dark green foliage. As compact, upright shrubs, they are well-suit-ed for the smaller garden. Portlands are relatively rare in that very few cultivars were introduced and fewer still are widely available today. Examples: 'Duchess of Portland' (1800), also known as the Portland Rose, forms semi-double, fragrant, bright beautiful red flowers on a 3-foot bush. 'Sydonie' (1846) has double, flat, fragrant rose-pink blooms and grows to 5 feet. 'Yolande d'Aragon' (1843) bears large, double, bright pink, fragrant roses on a 5-foot plant.

NOISETTE ROSES were first produced by a Charleston, South Carolina, rice planter around 1802. John Champneys grew a seedling that was a cross of the Musk Rose (*Rosa moschata*) and 'Old Blush,' which was newly introduced from Asia. He called his rose 'Champneys' Pink Cluster.' Champneys shared seeds and plants of his hybrid with a friend, Philippe Noisette, who realized the importance of the cultivar and sent plants

I*n the spring, the long, bowing canes of 'Gertrude Jekyll' are layered with heavy, fragrant blossoms.*

The cup-shaped flowers of 'Bow Bells' hark back to the classic form of the Bourbon Rose. They contrast nicely with the spearmint green of the foliage.

to his brother, a nurseryman in Paris. The brother introduced several cultivars in France, where they gave the new class of repeat-blooming roses the name Noisette. Early Noisettes were bushy shrubs with small flowers produced in large, elegant clusters similar to their Musk Rose ancestors. French nurserymen soon began producing hybrid crosses with Tea Roses, resulting in a line of large-flowered Climbing Roses. Most Noisettes are tender to cold yet are still very popular in the milder zones of the South and Southwest. Examples: 'Crépuscule' (1904) bears small, double, sunset-and-gold flowers that are fragrant and repeat well on a bush 8 feet in height. 'Lamarque' (1830), with large, double, fragrant white flowers with lemon tones, climbs to 12 feet. 'Mme. Alfred Carrière' (1879) has large, fragrant, globular, cupped, cream-and-pink blooms on a climber to 16 feet.

BOURBON ROSES originated on the Île de Bourbon (now Réunion) near Mauritius in the Indian Ocean. Before the opening of the Suez Canal in 1871, this island was a regular stop for ships traveling between Europe and the Far East. Bourbons are thought to have originated from an accidental crossing of the repeat-blooming China 'Old Blush' and the Damask 'Autumn Damask,' which were both grown by island colonists as field hedges in the early 1800s. A versatile group, Bourbons can be tall shrubs or climbers. Most repeat readily throughout the season. The blooms are more often cupped than rosette-shaped and produce a powerful Old Rose fragrance. Relatively hardy, they can be grown in most parts of the United States. Examples: 'Boule de Neige' (1867) has double, flat, fragrant white-pink blooms and grows to 6 feet. 'Mme. Pierre Oger' (1878) forms double, cupped, fragrant blossoms of white-pink edged with rose pink and reaches up to 8 feet. 'Souvenir de la Malmaison' (1843) produces lovely double, flat, fragrant pink flowers on a 3-foot plant.

HYBRID PERPETUAL ROSES

were the dominant class of roses through the late Victorian era, with over 1,000 cultivars having been introduced during that period. In America, most of the roses remembered from grandmother's garden as "cabbage roses" are actually Hybrid Perpetuals rather than Centifolias. Descended from about every class of Old Rose, the Hybrid Perpetuals were cherished for their ability to rebloom in cooler climates. Strong crimson, a color lacking in many earlier classes, is most often found among Hybrid Perpetuals. The tall, upright canes are well-suited for inward or outward pegging. The name is perhaps a bit optimistic in that Hybrid Perpetuals generally produce an outstanding spring bloom followed by an intermittent, rather than continuous, display later in the season. The earliest cultivars of Hybrid Perpetuals are the most dependable repeat-bloomers in this class. They are quite cold-hardy in much of the United States. Examples: 'Baronne Prévost' (1842) yields double, flat, quartered, deep pink, fragrant flowers that repeat, and grow to 5 feet in height. 'Enfante de France' (1860) has double, quartered, flat, fragrant silver-pink blooms, repeats well, and grows to 4 feet. 'Reine des Violettes' (1860), with fragrant, double, cupped violet-purple flowers, is a repeat-bloomer on a 4-foot bush.

MODERN ROSES

The advent of Modern Roses began with the introduction of Hybrid Teas. As a class, they differed very little from Hybrid Perpetual Roses until the inclu-

*S*trongly perfumed blooms of 'Leander' age to peachy pink, ruffled blooms reminiscent of antebellum petticoats.

sion of new genetic influences taken from a double yellow form of the species *R. foetida*. This allowed hybridizers to widen the color range of Modern Roses to include yellows and oranges. The first bright yellow Modern Hybrid Tea Rose, 'Soleil d'Or,' was introduced in 1900 by its hybridizer, Joseph Pernet-Ducher, and this opened the gates for the flood of yellow and orange roses that followed.

The modern Hybrid Tea Rose is defined more by the shape of the half-opened bud than by any other characteristic. Its distinctive, tightly pointed bud has been the standard of rose beauty for more than a hundred years. Among the best-known classes of Modern Roses are Floribundas, Grandifloras, Climbers, Shrubs, and Miniatures.

HYBRID TEAS are what we now regard as the traditional florist's rose—just think of every bouquet of long-stemmed roses you've ever given or received, each lone, pointed bud displayed at the tip of its stem. The bush, foliage, and prickles of Hybrid Tea Roses can vary greatly as they are the product of hybridizers' combining many different classes of roses to produce a particular flower form. Hybrid Teas are also less cold-hardy than many of their predecessors. Examples: 'Summer Sunshine' (1962) has double, bright yellow, slightly fragrant blooms on a 5-foot bush. 'Touch of Class' (1984) bears double, coral pink flowers with slight fragrance on an upright-growing plant to 6 feet. 'Olympiad' (1984), with double, bright red roses and little to no fragrance, grows to 5 feet.

F*or maximum effect, 'Sir Edward Elgar' can be planted in clusters of three bushes.*

FLORIBUNDAS flower in large clusters, with smaller individual blooms than those of Hybrid Teas. Bushes are usually 3 to 4 feet tall and work best in the garden when used at the front of a bed or border, or as hedges. Examples: 'Iceberg' (1958) forms clusters of fragrant, pure white blooms and grows to 4 feet. 'French Lace' (1982) bears very fragrant, ivory white flowers, one to twelve to a stem, on a 4-foot plant. 'Sun Flare' (1983) has large clusters of double, lightly fragrant, bright yellow blooms on a compact bush to 3 feet.

GRANDIFLORAS are not really encountered much as a group these days. Produced from a cross between Hybrid Tea and Floribunda Roses, Grandifloras produce their flowers in large clusters, like the Floribundas, and have the vigor and growth habit of the taller Hybrid Teas. Examples: 'Queen Elizabeth'

A *climbing French Rose, 'Eden' has been trained onto a lovely, rustic garden arch to blend with perennials and the bright pink of 'Charmian' (background).*

(1955), the first Grandiflora, with cupped, clustered pink flowers, grows to 6 feet. 'Olé' (1964) has flat, fragrant orange-red flowers and also grows to 6 feet. 'Mt. Hood' (1996) produces clustered white blooms on a 6-foot shrub.

CLIMBING ROSES are often sports, or mutations, from bush forms or, as in the case of Large-Flowered Climbers, hybridized from seed. Climbing Roses do not attach themselves to a structure, as wisteria and ivy do, but must be tied to a support. Climbing Roses come in all classes and flower forms, with most modern Climbers classed either as Climbing Hybrid Teas (Cl HT), which tend to be cold-sensitive, Climbing Floribundas (Cl F), or Large-Flowered Climbers (LCl). Examples: 'New Dawn' (LCl, 1930) bears delicately fragrant, pink fading to white roses on an extremely vigorous and very winter-hardy shrub that grows to

12 feet. 'Climbing Peace' (Cl HT, 1950), with lightly fragrant, double yellow to pink blooms, also grows to 12 feet. 'Altissimo' (LCl 1966) carries single (five to seven petals), beautiful blood red flowers with slight to no fragrance on an 8- to 12-foot shrub.

Our concept of what makes a rose has been influenced by what has gone before. Any standards set for roses are nothing but arbitrary rules we ourselves place on this family of plants. We carry around in our heads an image of what a "rose" is, and that image is just as artificial and arbitrary as anything can be.

Our Modern Roses are the end product of a very long process of human selection, and we fool ourselves if we think them the pinnacle of rose development. Years from now, our grandchildren will look back at the twentieth century and wonder what all the fuss was about over all those "quaint old pointy roses" grown way back when.

WHAT IS *an* ENGLISH ROSE?

English Roses have been around for about thirty years, but their popularity and distribution in the United States is a very recent phenomenon—only within the last decade have they become commercially available in American garden centers and nursery catalogs. This book and field guide offers information on how English Roses perform in the varied climatic areas around the United States, not in England, the home of their creation, where growing conditions can be quite different. But before we discuss the roses themselves, we need to look at the genius behind them, David Austin.

A widely held misconception about roses is that cultivars are produced in volume by growing them from seeds. Nothing could be further from the truth. Every plant of each rose cultivar for sale in the garden center descends from *a single seed*. Even the most scientific breeding programs in operation today still depend on growing a large volume of seeds from which hybridizers select a few plants for the commercial market. A hybridizer may grow as many as a quarter of a million seedlings a year, of which they may discard all but two or three for future introduction. The rose 'Peace,' which has recently celebrated its fiftieth anniversary and is one of the best known and loved roses of this century, was the chance product of one seed. The hybridizer, Francis Meilland, selected this plant from many out of his crop of seedlings. All subsequent 'Peace' plants have been produced by asexual methods, namely by grafting or by rooted cuttings. This means that each and every 'Peace' plant is identical to the first bush, a mirror image or clone, if you will, of the single mother plant. So when you

*A*lthough only a once-bloomer, the deeply cupped and marvelously fragrant flowers of 'Constance Spry' make quite an impact in the spring garden.

grow a cultivar of a historic rose in your garden, you actually have a piece of the original.

Most successful hybridizers are content to develop new roses that are more or less in the commercial mainstream of what the buying public finds acceptable. For almost a century, hybridizers have been inbreeding Hybrid Tea and Floribunda Roses to the point that their incestuous productions are no longer fit garden plants. They are leggy and stiff flower factories, the only apparent difference from plant to plant being the color of their flowers. It is as though most hybridizers are simply xeroxing the flowers and changing only the flower color from photocopy to photocopy. We gardeners are just now being given the choice between rose plants as flower-producers (which do have a place in our gardens) and a whole

new group of repeat-blooming shrub roses to incorporate into the landscape.

FATHER OF THE ENGLISH ROSE

David Austin has been at work developing his English Roses since the 1950s, and during this time he has introduced nearly 120 cultivars. He has literally leap-frogged the mainstream of rose hybridizing, creating a new class of roses and then developing a worldwide market for them. Almost single-handedly, he has taken the rose out of the rosery and brought it back into the garden. But perhaps Austin's greatest contribution to the world of roses is that he changed the public's conception of roses from bouquet factories to integral shrubs in the garden landscape. Tired of the one-note roses being produced, he created his new class by combining the best traits of the old and new.

Working from his family's farm in Shropshire, England, Austin wondered why the charm of Old Roses had been seemingly lost in favor of flower mills cranking out Modern Hybrid Teas. And so, in the '50s, he began hybridizing with the goal of modernizing Old Roses by improving their frequency of bloom. His first attempts entailed crossing once-blooming Old Roses with repeat-blooming Modern Roses to produce shrubs with the open growth habit, fragrance, and flower charm of the Old Garden Roses, and then combining those traits with the health and repeat-blooming power of Modern Roses. His first hybrids, however, were only once-flowering.

Austin's insight was to back-cross these early once-flowering roses with modern, repeat-blooming plants carrying more informal flower forms. This, in subsequent generations, produced repeat-blooming shrubs with old-fashioned styles of flower form. During the 1960s Austin's work was taken up with experimentation and early attempts to define his new class of English Roses. His first introduction was 'Constance Spry,' in 1961, followed by 'Chianti' in 1967 and 'Shropshire Lass' in 1968—all once-blooming cultivars.

In 1969, Austin introduced his first repeat-blooming hybrids: 'Canterbury,' a cross of the Hybrid Tea 'Monique' and 'Constance Spry' with an English Rose seedling, and 'The Knight,' produced from 'Chianti' and a repeat-blooming English Rose seedling. In 1970, Austin started his own mail-order nursery to facilitate the introduction and sale of his new line of roses. But it wasn't until 1983 that he grabbed the public's attention with his introduction of two roses: 'Graham Thomas,' with globular buttery yellow flowers, a combination unique among Old Roses and unmatched in Modern, and 'Mary Rose,' with pink flowers produced in such abandon that they hark back to the best of the nineteenth-century French Damasks.

Austin's second inspired insight was the realization that if he used only Modern Roses for hybridizing (to ensure repeat-bloom), he would soon lose the Old Rose charm of his flowers and shrubs. So every few generations, he back-crossed his productions with true Old Roses to reinforce the essential "Old Roseness" of his hybrids. As a hybridizer, Austin soon discovered that if he concentrated only on

Growing more like a Damask Rose, 'Mary Rose' has the advantage of blooming through the entire season.

one part of his goal, he could very easily lose sight of the bigger prize.

If the decades of the 1960s and '70s were spent in developing this new class of roses, the '80s were spent in defining the essence of English Roses. These roses are not Old Roses—they are every bit as modern as the newest Hybrid Teas on the market.

WHAT EXACTLY IS AN ENGLISH ROSE?

So far, English Roses have been defined by the eye of their hybridiz-er, David Austin. Since English Roses share no single breeding line, the first were produced by crossing selected Old Garden Roses with modern, repeat-blooming parents. Defining what constitutes an English Rose is much more subjective than defining other types of roses, and to date the designation "English Rose" has not been accepted by the rarefied world of organized rose societies. Because English Roses are neither wholly old nor wholly new, the American Rose Society placed them in the

WHAT'S IN A NAME?

In the eighteenth century, the Swedish botanist Carl von Linné, who published under the Latin form of his name, Linnaeus, developed the binomial classification system using the number and arrangement of sexual parts of plants for their classification. Up to his time, plants had been classified by long, complicated descriptions that used geographic location and other factors for identification. Linnaeus simplified all this by giving plants and animals just two names—a generic name and a specific name. After Linnaeus's time, this process was expanded in the scientific community, particularly in the area of biology, to include seven distinct classifications. Using a modified form of Latin as the basis for naming objects, individual specimens were charted by the seven identifying categories, with each amplifying the one before it. The complete list is as follows: kingdom, phylum, class, order, family, genus, species. Each of these divisions, in descending order, defines and describes the relationships of plants to one another, right down to Linnaeus's genus and species. Emphasizing only these last two categories for regular identification purposes became known as binomial classification.

To these categories, modern botanists have added variety and cultivar. The term *variety* denotes a naturally occurring slight variation of a particular species. The term *cultivar* denotes an artificial hybridization (and thus a cultivated variety), which can only be kept in cultivation by asexual propagation—in other words, it cannot be grown true-to-form from seed. Many object to the fabricated feel of this word, but cultivar has a very well-defined use and acceptance in botany. All Modern Hybrid Roses are cultivars in that they were produced by human activity: A hybridizer chose the parents, made the cross artificially, and out of the resulting batch of seedlings, selected one or more unique seedlings to be named for commercial sale.

T*he nodding, extravagantly fragrant flowers of 'Abraham Darby,' here trained onto a garden structure, simply demand that you stick your nose into them.*

rather nebulous, all-encompassing "Shrub" class.

But how do *we* classify these new roses of David Austin's? Should we fall in line behind the ARS, or should we perhaps make an effort to consider carefully David Austin's own view of his creations and invent a totally new classification for them? Getting two people to agree is difficult at best; getting everyone in a large, opinionated group to come to unanimous agreement is all but impossible. Rosarians are, on the whole, a cantankerous bunch, arguing for personal points of view long after any sensible need. Take, for example, the controversy over the acceptance of naming the Hybrid Tea class. Our old friend 'La France' was the first of its kind, but the class itself was not recognized by

the English Rose Society for nearly forty years after its introduction.

In like manner today, though the class "English Rose" is not yet an accepted designation, it is the name by which the rose-buying public identifies this group. It is, however, difficult to select uniform characteristics to define and describe the class. Austin's roses share very few common characteristics of parentage, flower form, or growth habit. One of the most unifying characteristics is the repeat-bloom, and even this is not universal—or unique—to his roses. In this area, however, he has been most successful, with the few exceptions coming mostly from his early work. 'Constance Spry' and 'Chianti' are two examples of once-bloomers that seem always to be

The fragrant blooms of 'Gertrude Jekyll' hold on to their shape both on the bush and in a bouquet.

FLOWER COLOR: Until very recently, the flower color of English Roses has, on the whole, remained on the strict pastel-and-primary side of the spectrum. The hottest of the orange and red tones, as well as the blends, have been avoided. Austin's avowed goal has been, if not to *remake* Modern Roses with the looks of classic Old Garden Roses, at least to attempt to produce roses that *blend* into those groups, which explains the range of hues he has stayed with to this point. This is not to say that in the future we will see only roses of old-fashioned hues in this class. Austin has just introduced one very bright, very bushy-tailed hot orange and yellow cultivar named 'Pat Austin.' He will probably want

included in rosarians' lists of favorite English Roses.

In order to make a case for the acceptance of the appellation "English Rose," it will be necessary to list characteristics that define an English Rose. Since Austin has used a broad range of parents to produce his new class, parentage, in and of itself, is not enough to identify this class.

FLOWER FORM. An English Rose is at its most perfect stage in full, open bloom, regardless of bud shape or number of petals. Single, semi-double, and fully double blooms are all included, along with cupped, pompon, and quartered bloom shapes. Modern Roses are cherished primarily for their bud form, but like the true Old Roses that English Roses emulate, it is the fully open stage of flower form that is considered most beautiful and desirable in this class.

SPORTS

Like a sudden, unexpected flick of a genetic switch, sports are spontaneous mutations that occur in rose cultivars. Often, major characteristics of the original are altered. The most common occurrence is that the color of the flower is modified, sometimes drastically. Other changes occur less frequently— most notably, a bush can sport to a climbing form, and sometimes a very double flower can sport back to a five-petaled flower. Such a mutation, called a variety if it has sported from a Species Rose, is the most common way new roses are produced *after* artificial hybridization. Sports themselves can be propagated only by asexual means—either as a grafted plant or as a cutting to be grown on its own roots.

to test this debutante to see if the buying public will welcome more zesty-colored offerings displayed on roses with old-fashioned shapes. There's a good chance they will. By and large, however, bloom colors will most likely continue to lean toward those hues that blend into the garden without clashing with the rest of the landscape. This trend will most likely remain the foundation of his new introductions for some time to come.

REMONTANCY. For the most part, the best, most desirable English Roses are those that bloom repeatedly throughout the year. The few equally good once-bloomers are the exceptions, as well as the forebears of the remontant ones. This aspect truly helps to set English Roses apart from the pack.

FRAGRANCE. Another fundamental trait of English Roses is their varied and powerful aromas. But a choice cultivar that is very fragrant to one of its fans may seem rather bland and scentless to another. And since there is no one fragrance that can be said to define an English Rose, this attribute alone cannot be seen as any sort of standard-bearer for the class. As a group, though, it must be said that English Roses are fragrant. Many say they are the most fragrant of all rose types, and truly, it is that rosy aroma we remember best when coming away from our favorite garden.

GROWTH HABIT. This should be one of the simpler qualities to define but, because Austin has used a wide and varied number of parents over the years to develop this

P *ink-flowered 'Mary Rose' here sports to the white-flowered 'Winchester Cathedral.'* *Sports are spontaneous mutations that happen from time to time on garden plants.*

The thorny canes and deep green foliage of 'Wenlock' give this English Rose the look of a classic Gallica Rose of yesteryear.

class, English Roses can be low growing, low and spreading, medium and bushy, and even tall and spreading in habit. The one unifying feature seems to be a shared habit of fountainlike shape. English Roses, no matter how tall or short, all share an open V-shape, with the canes growing in a somewhat wider than tall fashion. This habit makes the class very desirable as landscape shrubs, helping them blend into the rest of the garden so effectively. Most Hybrid Teas are rather upright, leggy, and stiff in habit, which makes them fit only for inclusion in beds of their own ilk. Some Floribundas, such as 'Iceberg,' possess this fountainlike growth property, making them good candidates for breeding analogous shrubs (as a matter of fact, 'Iceberg' is a chief parent in many of Austin's bloodlines).

OVERALL LOOK: This is by far the most subjective trait. "Does it look like an English Rose?" tends to be a difficult but significant defining question. In this definition, overall look is the totality of all the characteristics that go into making a rose an English Rose. Tall-growing or short, fully petaled, quartered, or five-petaled, remontant or once-flowering—an English Rose is, first and foremost, a rose designed to be placed within a landscaped garden, helping to create an integrated tableau where there were only individual rosebushes before.

What Roses Need *and* How *to* Provide It

Roses are very undemanding plants: Given sun, water, fertilizer, and basic care, they repay their stewards with armloads of perfumed blossoms. But read the books or listen to the experts who make something simple into a terribly complicated ordeal, and it's no wonder that so many new gardeners are turned off to the idea of rose growing. Growing healthy rosebushes is not a matter of following a list of complicated rules; nor is it a matter of becoming an investor in an international chemical company. For most of us, it's simply applying a few basic principles of horticulture.

For some time, it has been apparent that the more one could simplify caring for, pruning, and maintaining roses, the happier everyone, including the roses, would be. This is especially true of English Roses. The complex myths that surround rose growing are astonishing. The true education of a gardener comes not from reading books but from being in the garden. Make observations, experiment, and remember what works and what fails. Don't be confused by all the conflicting information surrounding rose growing, and remember just one rule: "Roses can't read!"

Especially when considering the space and size that a particular cultivar will reach, don't believe everything you read. For the most part, published statistics come to us from Great Britain, but English Roses tend to grow much larger in the United States than the

*S*elf-pegging the long canes of 'Charmian' will increase flower production to its *maximum potential.*

heights and widths listed in British catalogs. A good rule of thumb to remember when reading British catalog descriptions of new English Roses is that if the cultivar is listed as growing between 2 and 2½ feet, it will probably stay under 4 or 5 feet; if it is listed as growing 3 feet or more you're probably going to have a giant on your hands. While using David Austin's own descriptions on how large these roses grow, I realized that a number of mistakes had been made in my own garden—such as planting roses in the front of the border that grew far too tall for such placement. It still happens; last season, 'Brother Cadfael' was planted in front of a bed and is now over 10 feet tall!

The Austin nursery, on which growing conditions noted in his catalog are based, is located near Shropshire, England. Many areas of North America have longer grow-ing seasons and receive more regular doses of sun; longer seasons mean that the roses simply have more time to grow and will, if it's in their nature, grow taller than they would with a shorter growing season. There are regions—most notably the Pacific Northwest, the upper Midwest, and New England—with similar growing conditions to those of the United Kingdom, and in these regions, English Roses will perform as they would in their homeland. It's also important to note that nursery catalogs are written to describe a plant's growth during the first year or two, not the ultimate height and width it will achieve.

Most of us select a rose for the color of the flower, but there are other important considerations. Before you select a rose, you need to know how big the plant is going to grow and where it will fit in your garden. There are techniques that can be applied to help control rampant growth, but you must remember that a tall-growing rose-bush will always want to grow tall no matter how hard you try to keep it short.

After a cultivar's ultimate growth size, the next most important consideration is its health. Starting off with healthy cultivars will prevent a lot of trouble in the future. A universally "perfect" rose does not exist—while a specific cultivar will do fine in one region, it just might have a problem in another due to different growing conditions and weather. Selecting healthy, easy-to-grow cultivars is a matter of research. Look at your neighbors' gardens and make a field trip to a local rose-display garden, taking note of those roses that seem to be doing best under growing conditions similar to those of your own garden. Although one can learn a lot from catalogs, it is far more helpful to discover actual growing information from garden conditions that resemble yours. The information in this book has not been gleaned from other books or catalogs, but rather from experience and observations on growing English Roses in various parts of the country.

WHAT DO ROSES NEED?

Roses in general, and English Roses in particular, demand the basic requirements in order to grow and flower at their best: sun, soil, water, and food.

SUN. English Roses are no different from other roses; they are plants adapted to growing in direct sun-

light. A minimum of four to six hours of direct sun a day is required for the plant to grow and produce bloom. Although there are a few English Rose cultivars that will grow with less than optimum sun, they will flower less. Many English Roses have as one parent the Floribunda 'Iceberg,' which will grow and flower under less than ideal sun conditions. One rose with this ancestry is 'Graham Thomas.' It will tolerate as little as four hours of direct sun per day, but under these conditions, it will produce only about 50 percent of the flowers it would have produced with an optimum amount of sunlight.

Plants use sunlight to manufacture the sugars that go into driving their metabolic processes. Sunlight provides the energy to break down water molecules and recombine them with carbon dioxide from the atmosphere to produce the sugars necessary for plant life (try to

T*he buttery yellow color of 'Graham Thomas' is unique and unmatched by any other rose.*

remember that long-gone day in class when the teacher described photosynthesis). Flower production utilizes tremendous amounts of stored energy, and continuously blooming English Roses need as much direct sunlight as possible to drive their flower factories.

Selecting a site away from the direct competition of tree roots will also promote better bloom production. Most trees' roots grow underground to a length equaling that of their farthest-reaching branches, so you will want to select a site away from overhanging tree limbs for your roses. Not only will the branches shade the garden area, stealing away sunlight, but the tree roots will compete with the roses for available water and nutrients.

In some parts of the U.S.—most notably parts of the Southeast and much of the Southwest—roses can receive too much sun; in those areas, it might be desirable to select a rose garden site where the plants receive some midday shade or protection from the most intense sun. The Pacific Northwest and many coastal regions have prolonged periods of overcast, so in these regions selecting as sunny a site as possible will promote the healthiest and best-blooming roses.

SOIL. Soil is composed of inorganic, dead organic, and living organic matter, in addition to water and lots of air space. The three basic types of soil are clay, silt, and sand. Clay is composed of the smallest particles, measuring less than $\frac{1}{12,500}$ inch in diameter. Silt has a particle size of up to $\frac{1}{500}$ inch. Sand particles are the largest and measure from $\frac{1}{200}$ to $\frac{1}{12}$ inch.

PRESCRIPTION FOR IRON-POOR SOIL

Chlorosis, a plant condition observed as yellowing of leaves, is caused by a deficiency of available iron in the soil. Most soils have more than enough iron, but because of too-alkaline soil conditions, that iron can become unavailable to the plant's roots. To correct the problem, reduce soil alkalinity and use fertilizers with chelated iron. Iron that has been chelated is easily "digested" by your rose's roots and will continue to provide this essential element to the plant.

The best soils are made up of a mixture of inorganic or mineral and organic components. The two extremes of pure clay soils and pure sand soils require the most attention before planting can begin. Clay particles are so small that they tend to compact and close out most air space, while also retaining too much of the water that should percolate through it. Sand particles, on the other hand, are so large that there is far too much air space, allowing the water to drain through it too rapidly.

Heavy soils with a high clay content will need regular aeration and amending with organic matter. Any good commercial planter's mix or mulch will do, as will your own homemade compost. Just dig in the compost so that it is well mixed with the native garden soil. Light or sandy soils, on the other hand, will need amending with organic matter as well, although for a different reason. Adding organic matter in the form of compost or manure, which acts like millions of tiny sponges, will help retain soil moisture and provide roots with a more nutritious and healthy environment.

Amending both soil types with sufficient organic matter or well-rotted manure will, in the case of clay, help form clumps of the soil and organic matter to provide air penetration; combining sand with organic materials will allow far better water retention. One amendment quickens the water, the other slows it down, and both allow the all-important air pockets to be maintained. Silty soil, of course, is "just right."

Roses are not too demanding as far as soil goes; just about any well-draining soil will do. To test the drainage of your soil, dig a hole about the size of a shovel blade and fill it with water. Time how long it takes for the water to drain. If the hole empties in one hour or less, you have adequate drainage to grow roses. If the water takes longer than two hours to drain, it will be necessary to dig deeper or use a soil auger to penetrate through the barrier to promote adequate drainage. Or you could build raised beds—planting roses above the natural soil level will provide acceptable drainage. The most expensive solution to correct poor drainage is to install a French drain, (a perforated pipe placed in a gravel-lined excavation below the root zone) to carry away excess water.

A number of related soil problems are specific to certain regions of the country. Alkalinity tends to

'Abraham Darby' brightens up a woodland garden setting. Some English Roses will tolerate less than optimal sun and still grow and bloom.

go hand-in-hand with salinity. Alkaline and saline soils are usually found in regions with minimal rainfall, the desert Southwest and West, for example. Roses prefer a neutral to slightly acidic soil, the optimum being a pH around 6.5. Decomposing organic matter releases large amounts of organic acids and will help improve the pH of alkaline soils. Breaking up soil particles by amending the soil, which will also provide better drainage, allows salts to be flushed below the level of the plant's roots and will go a long way toward correcting any salinity problems.

Acid soils occur in areas with extensive rainfall. The water leaches calcium carbonate (lime) out of the soil, causing the soil pH to drop sharply. Additions of lime and/or soil sulfur will help correct this problem, bringing the pH back up to the 6.5 ideal.

A great deal has been written about soil preparation, soil acidity, and recommended additives. Just be aware that if you're not sure what the general soil conditions are in your area, you can always check with your state, county, or local agricultural adviser. All states maintain an agricultural advisory service through the state university system, and they can provide detailed information on local soil and growing conditions.

WATER. To grow and produce continuous flowers, it is absolutely essential that roses receive regular and adequate irrigation to maintain all that blooming power. How much and how frequently to water is a mystery to most gardeners. But for roses, the rules are

O*ne of the taller-growing English Roses, 'Charles Austin' can be self-pegged or pruned hard to encourage more bloom.*

actually quite simple. Rose shrubs require a regular supply of water to grow and produce flowers and should not be allowed to dry out between irrigations. In areas without regular and dependable rain, or during long dry spells, it will be necessary to irrigate the rose garden. Regular, deep applications of water are preferred over sporadic, shallow irrigations. Keep your soil type in mind when irrigating: Clay soils will need less frequent irrigation; sandy soils more.

If you live in an area that receives minimal rainfall, it will help to install an irrigation system. Many growers are shying away from simple overhead irrigation systems and selecting more complicated—but more efficient—drip systems. Drip systems allow water to soak in to the desired depth and apply the water to the root system of individual plants. These low-volume systems can save up to 50 percent or more on water usage.

Drip systems are more complex to install and maintain than other systems, and once you have installed an automatic system, you will need to check that it is in good working order on a regular basis. Because drip systems use small and rather fragile piping to deliver the water to the individual shrubs, they are much more vulnerable to damage and breakage from hoes, shovels, or other garden implements. Just stepping into the rose bed is enough to dislodge an emitter and direct the flow of water away from your precious English Roses. Constant monitoring is the key.

A less high-tech irrigation system, called Leaky Pipe, has recently been made available. Leaky Pipe

'The Dark Lady' will live up to its name only in cooler weather; the rest of the year it will be much paler.

utilizes a porous, hoselike pipe made from recycled rubber automobile tires. The Leaky Pipe hoses are arranged in the garden by weaving them through the base of the plants to deliver water at low pressure directly where it is needed. Leaky Pipe systems can rest on top of the soil or be covered by soil or mulch so that they are next to invisible; and because they are covered, the water they deliver will not evaporate as quickly. One must always keep in mind, though, that Leaky Pipe is vulnerable to damage in exactly the same ways drip systems are, although when cut, Leaky Pipe can be patched rather easily. It is also easy to put these low-volume systems on automatic watering timers. Simple mechanical dial timers, found in most garden centers and catalogs, connect to a hose attachment or faucet and work like a manual kitchen timer.

The brilliant crimson flowers of 'L. D. Braithwaite' last well when cut for bouquets or left on the plant to make a major statement in the garden.

Low-pressure systems such as drip irrigation and Leaky Pipe should be run long enough for the water to soak the plant roots thoroughly. Clay soils may require several hours to achieve this; in sandy soil areas, the task can be accomplished in a much shorter time. A significant loss of water from evaporation occurs during the hottest part of the day, so water at night or during the cooler parts of the day to reduce water evaporation and soil desiccation.

Overhead irrigation systems are less efficient, applying water over an entire area, not just where it is needed. Additionally, they must be used during the day to allow the blooms and foliage to dry before evening so that the onslaught of fungal diseases is minimized. Such systems can be modified to deliver water at soil level, and newer sprinkler systems are available with this alteration.

FOOD. Roses are greedy feeders. They require regular applications of a balanced fertilizer to encourage regular blooming. Commercial fertilizers come prepackaged and ready to apply, but you must know how to read the package to make an intelligent choice. Just like all food products available in the supermarket today, plant fertilizers, by law, must be labeled with specific information. All commercial fertilizers list the NPK ratios of the contents. NPK stands for nitrogen, phosphorus, and potassium (symbol K on the Periodic Table), the three most important plant nutrients. Depending on soil type and fertility, commercial fertilizers are formulated with differing ratios of NPK. Along with the listed ratios, the sources of each nutrient is listed. The actual amounts of NPK in the product are expressed in percentage of bag weight. For example: a 100-pound bag of a 14-10-6 plant product would contain 14 pounds of nitrogen, 10 pounds of phosphorus, and 6 pounds of potassium. This is an optimum standard ratio for roses. Keeping this formula in mind will help you make informed choices when you next purchase fertilizers for your roses.

The most important nutrient for almost all plants, including roses, is nitrogen. Nitrogen comes in soluble (or quick-release) forms, as well as insoluble (or slow-release) forms. Most commercial fertilizers contain the quick-release forms of nitrogen, but for roses it is desirable to find a commercial fertilizer that provides *both* slow- or timed-release *and* soluble nitrogen. Timed-release fertilizers will deliver regular and constant amounts of nutrients over a pre-programmed, three- to four-month period. The soluble nitrogen will give immediate vitality.

Products like cottonseed, blood meal, and bone meal are organic sources of nitrogen; urea and ammonium sulfate are inorganic sources. Plants are capable of absorbing nitrogen only in its most basic chemical form; they can do that with either, it just happens at different times. The inorganic types are absorbed immediately, but soil organisms must break down the organic forms before plants can absorb the nutrients. Organic fertilizers will simply take longer to become useful, especially during cool weather.

Once you've selected a good balanced fertilizer that has around 14 percent nitrogen or more, follow the package instructions for amounts and frequency of appli-

*M*ake your own garden vignette by training a climbing rose onto and over an old bird house. Here the Hybrid Musk Rose 'Lavender Lassie' has been used.

The large-growing 'Constance Spry' is here used as a hedge to divide one part of the garden from another, creating separate rooms.

cation. A slow-release, timed fertilizer will feed the roses for three to four months, providing them with a regular and constant supply of nutrients for maximum flower production.

What you use to feed your roses isn't as important as being consistent and following the package instructions. It is best to apply a timed-release fertilizer two to three times during the growing season, although by supplementing these slow-release feedings with shots of soluble, quick-release nitrogen just before bloom cycles, you will help to boost the roses into bloom.

Applying inordinate amounts of nitrogen will not promote more flowers but will cause more succulent growth, which is more susceptible to disease and insect infestations. The trick is to find the balance between not enough and too much.

CREATING YOUR GARDEN

Making a garden your own creation is as important to well-being as decorating the home that it surrounds. In a world fraught with isolation, speed, callousness, and rancor, our little garden plots are a refuge for our own humanness, a place to be at peace. We relish the opportunity to alter our surroundings not only to comfort ourselves but also, in the long run, to be an expression of who we are and what we're about. While some are content with "keeping up with the Joneses," others need that small space to recreate themselves in a world that seldom encourages individuality.

Having come to an understanding of what roses are, what they require to flourish, and what makes English Roses in particular so special, you're now ready to embark on the actual selection of roses and their placement in the garden. Gardens and gardening have evolved over the centuries, going through periods in which they are organized in a loose and haphazard manner, and at other times in a very structured and formal way. Although your garden may not be a Giverny, a Sissinghurst, or a Tuileries, you have just as much potential to create something, whether simple or elaborate, that reflects your own soul.

PURCHASING ROSES

These days, English Roses seem to be in such good supply that we have our choice of any number of sources. Roses can be purchased in two ways: container grown and bare root. Container-grown roses are available during much of the year, though in most cases the available assortment tends to be limited to those cultivars that have a well-established market among the

*T*he Tea Rose-like flowers of 'Dove' clothe the plant from the ground up. Allowed to drape over a low wall, the flowers are displayed to perfection.

buying public. The advantage of buying and planting container-grown roses is that they are often in bloom; you can see the flower on the bush right in the nursery, and you can then select the best plants out of the available stock. You will pay more for a container-grown rose than for a bare-root rose, and there will usually be a more limited selection than there would be earlier in the season.

Bare-root roses are available from mail-order catalogs and garden centers during the dormant season, which is anytime from January and February in the Southeast and Southwest to April and May in the colder regions of the country. When selecting bare-root plants in the nursery, check to see that they have at least three strong canes and a large root system. A good bare-root rose, once

planted, will grow and flower that same spring.

Once you have your bare-root roses, it is important to plant them as soon as possible. Although not recommended, a bare-root plant can be stored overnight in its original packaging. Sometimes the package takes longer than expected to arrive from the mail-order source, so the packaging may already be in a desiccated state. Occasionally, plants might get set aside after you get them home and then are forgotten until they've become almost completely dried out. Don't worry, though; roses can be revived by soaking them for a day or two in a bucket of water. No need to even use fancy vitamin products. Simply submerge the whole plant, *canes and roots,* in the water and let it bathe at least overnight. Recently, some friends who were leaving for

Europe the day their rose order arrived in the mail put their purchases in a bathtub filled with water and went off on their vacation. When they returned, two weeks later, they planted their roses without any die-off at all. Of course, it is best to keep new bare-root plants at their healthy best by planting them right away, but roses are tough when they need to be.

Selecting English Roses either from catalogs or a local garden center is more a matter of convenience than anything else. A catalog usually offers a wider selection of cultivars, while visiting a nursery gives you the advantage of personally inspecting and selecting your rose plant.

During the growing season, garden centers do offer some con-tainer-grown English Roses for sale, and the numbers and variety are increasing every year. These plants were received from the wholesaler as bare-root plants and were then potted up into containers for sale during the flowering season.

PLANTING

Planting an English Rose is really no different from planting any other rose. Some gardeners prefer to dig and amend the whole garden, while others just prepare and amend individual holes for each plant. Whether your soil is sand or clay, generous applications of well-composted organic material, mixed thoroughly into the planting soil, will be beneficial and give your garden a head start. Don't skimp on preparation—why pay up to $25 for a

GRAFTED VS. CUTTING-GROWN ROSES

Roses are propagated either by grafting or by cutting. A grafted rose is produced by joining (grafting) a selected scion onto a separate rootstock. The rootstock is started in the field as a cutting and allowed to grow for a year before the scion is attached.

Once grafted, the plant is allowed to grow for another year before it is dug up and offered for sale. A grafted rose has the advantage of having been given more time to grow, which often means you receive a larger, more vigorous shrub for planting.

Specialty mail-order catalogs and nurseries offer cutting-grown plants, often referred to as own-root, as an alternative to grafted roses. A cutting-grown rose is produced by taking a flowering stem of a cultivar and encouraging that stem to produce roots on its own. The complete plant you receive is the cultivar you selected, roots and all. A rose grown from a cutting will never produce suckers in the garden because it is entirely one cultivar. Cutting-grown roses have another advantage in that they will be free of rose mosaic virus, a nonlethal but disfiguring plant virus, as long as the cutting was taken from a healthy mother plant. Grafted plants need not be infected with the virus as long as the grower used virus-free rootstock and scions to start the plant. A cutting-grown rose, though, may be smaller than a grafted bare-root rose and take an extra year to catch up with the larger, grafted plant.

GRADING BARE-ROOT ROSES

The American Association of Nurserymen have set up grading standards for all bare-root roses sold in the United States. Following are the basic descriptions and interpretations of that information:

GRADE #1. *Roses in this grade are of the best quality. They must have three canes that start within 3 inches of the bud union. Canes of Grade #1 Hybrid Teas must be at least 18 inches long, and Floribunda canes must be at least 15 inches in length.*

GRADE #1½. *This grade requires two canes of 15-inch length for Hybrid Teas, and 14-inch-long canes for Floribundas.*

GRADE #2. *Roses in this grade require two 12-inch canes and, for the most part, are not recommended for consumer sale or planting.*

Most U.S. growers and nurseries are quite demanding in grading #1 bare-root roses, to the point that the stock for sale is almost always well above the minimum requirement. On the whole, you will receive very well grown, healthy, and strong bare-root roses from suppliers based in the U.S.

Own-root roses are not subject to a grading system. You should expect a smaller but equally healthy plant with a strong, fibrous root system. The plant should be ready to place into your garden upon receipt.

---

rosebush and plant it in a 50¢ hole? Remember that the rose you are planting will probably want to stay in that same spot for a number of years. Good basic horticulture dictates that the planting site be worked through with organic compost and provided with all the nurtrients necessary for healthy plant life.

Space large-growing English Roses with at least 3 to 5 feet between plants to allow them to grow and not compete for air space and sunlight. Adequate spacing promotes healthier plants by ensuring each plant gets enough sunlight, and the free movement of air around the plants will help discourage diseases and pests.

In the coldest parts of the country, plant roses with the bud union around 3 inches below soil level; this helps protect the tender growth point from freezing. In milder regions, plant the bud union so that it just rests on top of the soil. In both cases, new growth will be produced more symmetrically so that canes grow all around the bush, not just from the side with the bud union. Own-root, or cutting-grown, roses are planted at the same depth as they were planted in their pots. In areas exposed to heavy winds, plant your roses somewhat deeper in order to anchor the plant more firmly into the soil—you don't want tumbleweed roses blowing down the lane!

CONTAINERIZED ROSES. Prepare a planting hole approximately 2 feet across by 2 feet deep. Mix the native soil removed from the planting hole with an equal amount of compost or commercial

*I*n the corner of this perennial border, 'The Countryman' displays its old-fashioned charm to perfection.

planter's mix. Blend the soil/compost mix well. It isn't necessary to use a fertilizer when planting new roses; in fact, too much fertilizer will burn tender new roots and can actually cause the plant to die. However, if you feel you must add a fertilizer at planting time, use a timed-release type at half the recommended rate. No matter what the container, remove it before planting the rose. Place the new plant in the hole so that it will be at the proper planting depth when finished, and shovel in the soil/compost mix, firming it around the roots. Avoid air pockets by firming the soil around the base and roots with your hands and then step around the newly planted rose to firm in the soil/compost mix. Build a ring or water basin of soil around the newly planted rose to hold water. Fill the basin three times with water, letting each filling drain, to fur-

ther diminish any air pockets as well as to ensure that the roots are well soaked. If you notice a continuing stream of many air bubbles, there's an air pocket in the soil. Let the water drain and then firm the soil again by tamping down either with the shovel handle or with your foot. This should force soil into the air pocket. Once all the air pockets are gone, resume watering until the basin has filled and drained three times. Keep a close check on newly planted container-grown roses to make sure they do not dry out. Water as often as necessary; you can even sprinkle the canes with water on hot, dry days.

BARE-ROOT ROSES. To plant your bare-root rose, dig a hole to accommodate the roots of the new plant with several inches to spare—at least 12 to 18 inches deep and 12

PREFERRED ROOTSTOCKS

U.S. rose growers use one of several rootstocks for grafting. The most common rootstock used is the Old Rose cultivar 'Dr. Huey,' which has been selected for its compatibility with most other rose cultivars as well as for its uniform root growth and reasonable winter-hardiness. Some gardeners may want roses grown on seedling *Rosa multiflora* rootstocks, as this species has a much higher tolerance of severe winters. In some parts of the Southeast and West, 'Fortuniana' is the preferred rootstock because of this species' ability to tolerate the salty, alkaline soils sometimes found in those regions.

Placed in the informal setting of a cottage garden, the pure white flowers of 'Francine Austin' contrast beautifully with splashes of brilliant scarlet Oriental poppies.

inches wide. Amend the removed soil as explained above. Cut back any damaged roots and broken canes.

Form a mound of soil mix in the middle of the hole to support the roots. If the rose is grafted, position it so that the bud union is 2 to 3 inches below the soil level in cold-winter areas, or just resting at soil level in mild-winter areas; if self-rooted, the crown should be placed so that it is just at or slightly below soil level, depending on your climate. Spread the roots down over the soil mound and fill in the hole with your amended soil mix. Firm in the soil around the roots to eliminate any air pockets, and build a ring of soil around the newly planted bush to form a watering basin. Fill the basin with water three times, checking for air pockets as described above. If the weather at planting

time is hot and dry, you should protect newly planted bare-root roses by covering the canes with moist soil or mulch. Cut out the bottom of a brown paper shopping bag and place the bag over the new plant. Use moist soil or compost to fill the bag and cover the canes; after two weeks or so, you can remove the bag and soil. By that time, the plant should be strong enough to withstand extremes in weather and will be well on its way to producing flowers. Occasionally a bare-root rose will take its time breaking dormancy and leafing out, and this same brown-bag technique can be used to help the reluctant bare-root rose into growth.

Make sure newly planted roses are kept moist while they are settling in during the first few weeks. The new plants are growing roots and will need all the help they can get. As with container-grown roses, you can sprinkle the canes with water on hot, dry days to help keep them cool.

COMPANION PLANTING

We are just beginning to come out of the Victorian mindset that relegated roses to their own corner of the garden with nothing but canes and dirt to show for most of the year. English Roses are spearheading the return of rose "integration." Every size, texture, and shape of garden plant can be mixed together to complement one another when using English Roses.

Why not plant herbs and perennials and annuals in the rose garden? Or the other way around—plant rose shrubs in your perennial garden or herb border. English Roses can grow and mix well anywhere in your garden and their fountainlike growth patterns welcome other plants growing through and around them.

The art of gardening is to experiment, to try new things. Mixing colors and textures of other families of plants in the garden is once again popular, and the line between the rosary and perennial border need not exist. The possibilities are endless and up to you to discover what's right for you and your garden. Start with some simple, familiar plants you know from your local garden center. Plant a ground cover of lemon-scented thyme under your roses. When you work in the rose bed, the fragrance of roses will mix wonderfully with the scent of the lemon thyme. If you want something tall and spiky next to a low-growing rose, plant delphiniums nearby. To mix textures, try lamb's ears (*Stachys byzantina*), for its woolly silver-white foliage, next to the dark green foliage of 'The Prince.' The velvet-textured foliage of the lamb's ears will create a startling combination with the deep purple-crimson of the English Rose. In the colder regions, take advantage of the natural winter-hardiness of spring-flowering bulbs. Plant cream-and-pink Asiatic lilies with 'Cottage Rose' or underplant with red-and-white-striped lady tulips (*Tulipa clusiana*). Create height in the garden by training 'Sir Clough' up a pillar or over an arch and mixing in a contrasting clematis like one of the purple-blue *Clematis viticella* hybrids or a Jackmanii clematis. Both flower on new wood, so when you prune your roses, the clematis also gets a severe pruning just as buds begin to swell. Contrasting foliage textures and colors work well: Plant green-and-white-variegated hostas at the

'*Abraham Darby*' spilling out over a garden path creates a focal point in the small garden.

base of Austin's yellow-flowered 'Symphony,' and add some black-flowered pansies along with the spiky, white-flowered veronica 'Iceberg.'

In milder regions, contrast the buttery yellow flowers of 'Graham Thomas' with the tallest spikes of navy blue delphiniums and pull together this composition with mounds of gray-foliage dianthus. A shockingly brilliant combination can be created with the orange-apricot flowers of the Austin rose 'Tamora' and oriental poppies interplanted with colorful, repeat-blooming tall beared iris. If you don't use chemicals in your garden, then why not plant borders of crispy-leaf lettuces and deep purple opal basil around your roses?

The tall, white-flowered butterfly bush (*Buddleia asiatica*) planted with the soft lilac-pink flowered 'Charles Rennie Mackintosh,' complemented with hollyhock and hardy phlox, would create an informal cottage garden setting. Don't overlook the old standbys—annuals such as pansies, petunias, and marigolds to fill in those blank spots that appear in the summer.

Hide the lower canes of tall-growing English Roses, like the startlingly fragrant 'Gertrude Jekyll,' with the grasslike foliage of yellow-flowered daylilies. In those dark, shady spots under your taller English Roses, tuck in a clump of coral bells; the low mounds of scalloped-edged foliage and the wiry flowering stems will add interest and texture to that part of the garden.

Many people new to gardening avoid planting anything under their rosebushes, but ground-covering plants will help keep out weeds and give color and texture to the landscape. An often overlooked ground cover is the gray foliage and white flowers of the wide-spreading perennial snow-in-summer (*Cerastium tomentosum*). Plant snow-in-summer under the brilliant red of the Austin rose 'L. D. Braithwaite,' or use it as a border along a garden path planted with a hedge of pink-and-coral-flowered 'Lilian Austin.'

*T*he low-growing 'Symphony' should not be overlooked as it is one of the best of the yellow-flowered English Roses.

GROWING ENGLISH ROSES IN CONTAINERS

Given an appropriate-size container, most any English Rose will grow happily and flower in a pot. It is wisest, however, to select one of the shorter-growing cultivars to grow in a standard 12- to 14-inch pot. This convenient size will allow enough root growth to support one of the smaller cultivars well.

To plant a bare-root rose or a small-container rose in a pot, you need a good grade of commercial potting soil. Make sure you use potting soil instead of soil from your garden because the growing medium must be light and well draining to ensure a balance of air and water.

Place the rose in the center of your container, making certain that the final soil level will be 2 or 3 inches below the rim of the pot. Use your hands to work the potting soil around the roots in order to eliminate any air pockets. Do not compact the soil too much, though. Water the new rose well, and keep it moist until new growth is around 3 inches.

Feed your potted rose with a liquid fertilizer, used at *half* the recommended strength, about every other week through the flowering season. Make certain the roots never dry out completely. Check to see if the rose needs water simply by poking your finger 2 inches down into the planting medium to feel if it is moist; if it isn't, you need to water again.

Every other year, remove the rose from the pot, and using a garden knife or a sharp pair of pruners, trim off 3 inches of soil and roots from both the sides and bottom of the soil mass. Add the same amount of new commercial potting soil as was removed. Replace the soil mass, tamp it down lightly, and water thoroughly. With care, your container-grown roses should flourish and flower for many years to come.

Place a small plastic pond in the garden and plant a clump of 'Francine Austin' so that the long, arching canes, gray foliage, and huge clusters of small white flowers are reflected by the placid waters. Mix in clumps of pink false dragonhead (*Physostegia virginiana*) and blue pincushion flower (*Scabiosa caucasica*).

Extend the blooming season of your garden by planting deciduous flowering magnolias such as *Magnolia stellata* or *M. kobus,* both extremely cold-hardy varieties. The magnolia will flower in late winter or early spring and act as an alarm clock to announce the coming rose season. Lilacs planted to the back of the border will flower just before the roses, with both spreading their beauty and fragrance across the garden.

Create a bold architectural effect with the gray-green foliage and startling chartreuse flowers of *Euphorbia characias* ssp. *wulfenii;* the tall spikes of flowers will make quite a statement when contrasted with the peachy apricot, powerfully fragrant English Rose 'Evelyn.'

Don't overlook the informal

The pink Mexican evening primrose is here used to great effect, filling in around the base of the tall-growing English Rose 'Graham Thomas.'

nature of single-flowered English Roses like 'Moonbeam.' Mix her with clumps of purple-blue balloon flowers (*Platycodon grandiflorus*), add some sidalcea 'Elsie Heugh' in softest tones of pink, and underplant the group with the maidenhair-like foliage and blue-and-white flowers of dwarf columbine (*Aquilegia flabellata*). A tall English Rose hedge of 'Dapple Dawn' could use a low border of spiky-flowered blue veronica to cover up the lower canes, and the five-petaled pink flowers of the rose will look like a flight of butterflies has settled into your garden for a long stay.

Color complementing is a matter of personal preference rather than accepted precedent. If you think a magenta tulip looks nice growing next to an orange rose, enjoy. It might actually look great and be something no one else would ever have thought would work together. Maybe that variegated grass complements the dark black-purple-red of your Austin rose 'The Prince' to such great effect in one corner of your garden that you want to add a mirror image of the combination in the opposite corner.

What works for you, works! If, in the end, you decide it doesn't, you can always move the offending plant and try it somewhere else in the garden. Try blue flowers next to red roses, or maybe white roses in front of dark green foliage. Experiment with colors you would not normally mix together. Rules are made to be broken—the only rules you need to keep in mind are the basics of horticulture: Does the plant grow in sun or shade? Will it need more or less water than the rose? After that, the sky's the limit. Successfully mixing companion plants with roses in a garden setting takes imagination, color sense, and a little bit of luck.

Growing Roses Is Simple

Growing healthy roses is really not all that difficult. The major obstacle any rose grower must overcome is the years of brainwashing we have all received from the so-called experts. Most rose books emphasize the difficulties: weeds, insects, disease. While problems do exist, they are, for the most part, cosmetic and easily overcome with simple basic horticultural practices.

All the complex rules to the contrary, roses are very simple plants to grow. One problem for us in this country is that most of the books written on rose growing are based on British conditions and traditional methods. It has proved difficult for the American gardener to adapt this information to the different and varying regional conditions we encounter here.

For many years, rose experts have convinced us that growing healthy roses requires copious quantities of highly toxic chemicals to keep "Nature" at bay, when the truth is much more simple and straightforward. Well-grown roses contain within themselves the ability to throw off diseases and other biological attackers. When we resort to harsh chemical interventions, we are increasing our garden's dependence on artificial means of protection. Wide-spectrum chemicals affect not only the specific targeted problems but also destroy beneficial systems. This cascade effect is ongoing and simply increases our reliance on easy fixes.

Successful amateur rose growers know that a healthy, well-grown rose will repulse most problems and continue to flower on its own. An effective gardener takes advantage of the regional conditions he finds in his garden and, with good garden sense, selects cultivars adapted to his region. Horticulture is no mystery: If a rose is provided with good soil and adequate sun and water, spaced properly, and given simple care, it will flourish with ease.

MULCHING AND WEEDING

The most effective system of weed prevention is to use 2 to 3 inches of surface mulch to prevent weed seeds from germinating. An organic mulch is much more aesthetic and, of course, doubles as a soil amendment, but inorganic products such as lava rocks can be used as well.

Mulching has benefits other than just weed prevention. A thick layer of mulch will lessen evaporation and keep moisture in the soil, conserving water usage. Organic mulches will also break down and help improve soil texture as they are cultivated into the ground. Just keep in mind that mulches need periodic replacement because they break down and meld with the rest of the soil.

These days, chemical weed control for the garden entails the use of two types of systems: preemergence preventatives and spot killers. Before applying preemergence controls, existing weeds must first be removed; then, following instructions, the chemical is applied. Timing is all-important; these products must be applied just before the seeds of the target weed germinate. Spot weed killers are sprayed directly onto the target weed. Care must be taken not to allow any chemical to reach non-target plants as they will be damaged. Chemical weed controls may build up in the soil and have long-term affects on the soil's fertility and on plant health.

PRUNING

English Roses are no different from any other class of rose when it comes to pruning. Several styles of rose pruning will work, so choosing a pruning system is a matter of personal preference along with what goals you have for your roses. Rose shrubs don't really have to be pruned; if left unpruned, they will continue to grow and flower. In the wild, Species Roses are, of course, never pruned, except by freezes or the occasional deer. So why prune?

In the coldest regions of our country, it is necessary to prune the bushes back in order to protect the most tender cultivars from freezing. In the warmest zones, it is necessary to prune roses to force them into winter dormancy. For most gardeners, pruning roses helps to bring vigorous growth under control and contain the plants to a

CUTTING FLOWERS

When cutting blooms for the house, harvest either early in the morning, when it is still cool and the flowers are at their freshest, or later in the evening, when some moisture has returned to the air. Recutting stems under water will also help flowers last longer. Conditioning the cut flowers by placing them up to their buds in warm water overnight will help the blooms last even longer. The use of a flower preservative can help an arrangement last for a prolonged period; if you don't have a commercial flower preservative, try adding two or three ounces of regular (not sugar-free) lemon-lime soda to the water. The acid of the soda will help keep bacteria from blocking the water vessels in the rose stems and the sugar will feed the flower.

*T*he dependable repeat-blooming 'Mary Rose,' named for Henry VIII's sister, is rightly one of the most popular of English Roses.

workable garden size. It is also instrumental in controlling and maintaining the desired shape of each plant. A balanced, moderate pruning also focuses the rose's energies on flower production.

Choosing when to prune your English Roses is more a matter of where you live than just about any other factor. In the mildest areas of the United States, you will want to start pruning roses as early as the first of January; in the coldest areas, you may not want to begin pruning until March or April. Generally, in the colder regions, you will want to hold off on pruning roses until after the last chance of frost. Keep a lookout for pruning demonstrations offered by your local rose societies, botanical gardens, or garden centers to help you decide when is the best time for you to prune. Even the most experienced gardener can pick up new tips at these programs.

Pruning also activates the growth cycle built into the roses. After the shrub is pruned, chemical processes are initiated that cause the dormant plant to produce tender new growth. This tender growth can be adversely affected by a sudden freeze to the point of being killed, so timing is important.

At each break of a rose leaf on a cane, there lies a growth bud (also known as a leaf joint, or bud eye), which essentially lies inactive as long as the terminal growth point is above it. Once that top growth area is pruned away, whichever growth bud is nearest the topmost point of the cane will be the one that receives the chemical instructions to break into the growth cycle.

If you leave a section of non-growing cane behind when you prune, that portion of the cane will simply (and always) die back to the first growth bud available to receive the growth instructions.

Occasionally, that dieback doesn't stop at the first bud eye and you will sometimes lose entire canes. It is safest to find an outward-facing bud eye going in the direction you prefer and prune a horizontally angled cut just slightly above that bud eye. This way, there are no mixed signals for the growth of that particular cane.

There are some basic guidelines for how, and how much, to prune. We'll go through each step thoroughly so the process is clear. Remember, if an English Rose grows to 6 feet and you prune it back to 6 inches, the shrub will expend all of its energy growing back to its 6-foot height and will have very little left to produce flowers.

If a cane or branch is dead, it's dead—it won't ever come back. Pruning out dead growth simply helps tidy up the plants and creates room for new, healthy growth. Dead or diseased wood is just a potential source of infestation, and removing it will help suppress the spread of problems. Some English Roses are subject to natural dieback, a condition where a cane will start dying from the tip, continuing down the cane until the entire cane is dead. It can be caused by any number of problems; the only solution is to cut off the diseased portion of the cane just below the point where the tissue is still healthy.

When canes cross one another through the center area of the plant, not only does it cause crowding at the expense of bloom, but the thorny canes rubbing against one another *can* eventually expose sensitive underwood on one or both canes, thereby opening the entire plant to dieback, disease, and pests. In these cases, dead or

The long canes of the huge cupped flowers of 'Othello' can be trained up and over, arching to cross a garden path.

dying canes become waste material and are dangerous to the health of the rest of the plant. If the damaged canes are not removed, the sickness can eventually lead to the death of the entire plant. The best remedy, of course, is to redirect all the canes away from one another from the very beginning.

Most English Roses naturally have a V-shaped, or open, fountainlike growth pattern. Opening up the center of these cultivars will not require as much pruning as some of the larger English Roses, which produce many basal canes. Once a rose has been growing for three years or so, it is a good idea to renew the shrub by removing some of the oldest canes. A cane will continue to grow and flower for a number of years, but after three years, its best flower production will be over. So for each new cane produced by a mature shrub, you can remove one old cane. This helps keep the shrub to a controllable size and maximizes flower production by encouraging the production of new flowering canes. There is no hard-and-fast rule on just how many canes to leave after pruning. Garden space and personal preference will indicate how many canes you leave.

Most rose books recommend a much harder pruning than one-third to one-half, as I have, but it is clear from my years of experience that harder pruning simply limits the number of flowers the bush will produce. The question to ask yourself is "What do I grow roses for?" If the answer is "Flowers," then a light to moderate pruning will give you that result. If you prefer a particular *size* bush with

CREATING COMPOST

Composting garden trimmings, grass, and leaves will help reduce landfills and recycle plant waste back into the garden. Bacteria and fungi naturally break down dead plant matter, and by composting we are able to speed up these natural processes to our benefit.

A simple composting system consists of placing garden wastes in a heap, keeping it moist, and turning the compost regularly to promote the natural breakdown of the organic material into usable compost. Adding a handful of nitrogen fertilizer (either organic or chemical) to each layer of new plant clippings will promote bacterial activity, and the composting material will break down much faster. Keep compost moist to the touch but not saturated. Stirring the pile mixes in air and keeps returning the uncomposted outer layers back toward the center of the mix where the bacteria can do their work. A compost pile may reach 130 degrees Fahrenheit or more, even on a cool day. That's hot enough to kill most weed seeds, insects, and diseases.

You can find all sorts of composting devices in the garden centers and catalogs, but a good old backyard mound works just fine.

few flowers, you can do a heavy pruning to achieve that goal.

Some years back, an experiment was performed in several rose gardens. Three gardens with very different pruning systems were selected. One garden was pruned in the old traditional manner, cutting the roses back to under 12 inches; one garden was pruned to around 18 inches; and in the third garden, only about one-third to one-half of the previous year's growth was pruned. The experiment was followed up by regular visits to each garden to tally the number of buds and blooms. At first bloom, the traditionally pruned garden produced an average of six flowers per bush; the roses of the garden pruned at 18 inches produced around twelve flowers each; and the lightly pruned rosebushes of the third garden were each counted carrying over 150 flowers and buds!

Always prune to an outside-facing bud. Remember that the direction the bud faces is the direction in which the new shoot will grow. Pruning to outward-facing buds directs new growth away from the crowded center of the plant and out into the light, where it will receive more sun and thus will have that much more strength to produce ample flowers. When pruning or deadheading, make the cut just above a leaf joint; this is where the new flowering shoots will grow. Make the cut as close to the growth bud as possible without damaging it. Remember, don't leave stubs by cutting in between the leaves.

While you are pruning, be sure to remove any foliage left on the plant to make sure that the bushes get a full winter's rest. In cold areas, this will not be a problem as the leaves will have dropped off naturally. But in the warmer, temperate areas, where roses are pruned so early, there will be lots of

ROSE PRUNING IN 10 EASY STEPS

1. Cut off all dead and diseased wood.

2. Remove all crossover branches.

3. For each new cane produced, you can remove one old cane. This keeps only the strongest new canes for the new blooming season. These are always the best flower-producers.

4. Prune to about one-third to one-half of the last year's growth.

5. Cut to outside-facing buds. This directs new growth away from the center of the plant.

6. If they haven't fallen off on their own, remove all remaining leaves. This will initiate the important dormant cycle of the plant.

7. If necessary, seal pruning wounds larger than the diameter of a pencil with white glue.

8. Clean up around roses, removing all prunings and old leaves.

9. Remove all suckers from the areas around grafted plants. This should also be done year-round as suckers sap power from the rest of the rose.

10. Use a dormant spray to control overwintering pests.

leaves attached to the branches. Removing overwintering foliage will also help remove dormant disease spores and insect eggs. This doesn't mean that you will have eliminated all disease; it simply will curtail reinfection from your own plants.

'Pretty Jessica' grows low and produces crops of fragrant, long-stemmed blooms for cutting. One of the lowest-growing English Roses, it can be grown in a container.

In some climates, it is necessary to use a pruning or sealing compound on the larger pruning cuts. Sealing canes protects them from fungus, and especially from insects that lay their eggs on the open wound. The eggs hatch into larvae, which eat their way down the center of the cane, causing its eventual death. In some parts of the country, it is not as imperative to seal canes because pruning takes place so early that the insects are not yet active and the roses have the chance to heal on their own before there is any danger of infestation. But when in doubt, seal.

It is no longer recommended that you use commercially available pruning sealants found at most garden centers. These tar-based compounds contain chemicals that are toxic to the rose cane, often causing its death soon after application, and occasionally contributing to the premature death of the entire plant. You can seal wounds with a common product found in most households: white glue! White glue is nontoxic and comes in a handy applicator package. Just squeeze a drop of white glue onto every cane you've cut that's larger than the diameter of a pencil. The glue will dry clear and protect the open wound until the cane has had time to heal. Because the white glue dries clear, you may find you can't tell which canes have been sealed and which have not. In that case, just mix a drop or two of food coloring into the glue and you will eliminate this problem.

*A*ustin selected the name 'The Herbalist' because its semi-double blooms bear such *a strong resemblance to the Old Gallica 'Apothecary's Rose.'*

After pruning and sealing wounds, it's time to clean up the garden. Garden sanitation is just as important as keeping a home clean. Many insects and fungal spores spend the winter hidden in the litter and decomposing organic matter under our rosebushes. Some winter on weeds. You'll go a long way toward completing your preventive maintenance if you remove all weeds and rake up leaves and spent flower petals, putting them into the compost. As noted, a healthy compost pile will heat up to 130 degrees Fahrenheit or more, which is hot enough to kill insects and disease spores.

A big part of garden cleanup is the application of a dormant/cleanup spray after pruning is completed. Dormant sprays are used to eliminate overwintering disease or insects that might be on the plant. Two types of dormant sprays are available, and each has a very low toxicity rating. The first type, and the one that has been around the longest, is called Bordeaux mix. Made from lime and sulfur, these two substances act together to eliminate any overwintering diseases. The second type of dormant spray is made from oil and copper. The oil suffocates any insects and their eggs, while the copper acts as a mild fungicide. Either product will need a second, follow-up application about two weeks after the first application. Follow the label instructions for how much of either product to mix with water and use a tank or sprayer that attaches to a hose to soak the canes, bud union, and soil beneath the roses. Cleanup sprays will not guarantee a problem-free garden next season, but at least the chance of reinfestation from your own plants is greatly reduced.

If the fungus known as rose rust (sometimes simply referred to as rust) has been a particular problem, you can add a specific rust control to the oil-based dormant spray and then follow the directions. (If you don't want to use powerful chemical fungicides, leaf removal and an application of a dormant cleanup spray is a very good alternative.)

Don't let the idea of pruning daunt you. Just get out there and try it. You'll find, as many gardeners have, that once you start, you develop a certain joy in the doing (almost like harvesting), as well as a deeper connection with your garden through the process of reshaping your plants. It all goes back to that very primal instinct we have to dig our fingers into the soil, moving dirt and plants where we see fit, making our own creation out of the raw materials.

Experience is always the best teacher. Be patient with yourself, and know that the instinct to live and grow is deeply seated in all living things. You would have to work extremely hard to kill your beloved English Roses. Remember, they tend to grow and flourish more in *spite* of what we do to them than because of it.

TRAINING

One problem, especially with tall-growing English Rose cultivars, is how to promote repeat bloom and, at the same time, control the vigorous-growing shrubs so they will fit into gardens with limited space. You may want to consider self-pegging these roses, which will encourage the dormant buds all along the cane to break and produce flowers instead of just the bud at the tip.

Self-pegging is actually just a slightly more modern, technolog-

The lusty growth of 'Gertrude Jekyll' can be self-pegged to prevent the shrub from growing too tall.

ical version of a very ancient agricultural practice known as pegging. Simply bend the tall canes over and tie them to other canes on the same plant. Use soft, stretchable, green garden tape so that the tie does not cut into the canes and cause problems. This is much the same technique used with climbing roses. When the growth tip is below the rest of the cane, hormones produced in the tip are trapped by gravity and cannot move upward to get out into the cane. This enables every dormant bud eye to break into a flowering shoot. Instead of producing only one or two clusters of flowers at the tip, each self-pegged cane will produce fifteen to thirty or more clusters of blossoms along the entire length of the cane.

Self-pegging also permits us to grow the larger-growing English Roses in small urban or suburban gardens. A rose normally reaching 12 feet by 12 feet occupies 144 square feet. By self-pegging, it's possible to tame that same unwieldy rose into growing within as little as 24 square feet. You can potentially save six times the space occupied per rose and increase flower production by up to thirty times.

Another technique that promotes the popping open of dormant buds is to build a tripod of garden stakes and to tie the rose around the tripod. This system creates a lovely swirling effect with the canes that can, when in full bloom, make the roses look like they're spraying out from a fountain. The long, lax canes of some English Roses can also be bundled up and tied to a single stake to about two-thirds their length, so

that the end of the canes arch out, creating a cascading (or weeping) tree rose effect.

DEADHEADING

Deadheading is removing spent flowers and hips to enhance the shrub's appearance and to promote more bloom. If the hips are allowed to remain on the plant after the flowers die, a repeat-blooming cultivar will produce seed at the expense of flowers. Regular deadheading can also help control the growth of some of the larger-growing English Roses. And some English Rose cultivars are prone to dieback when the flowers are left on the shrub too long after they have finished.

When removing spent flowers and hips, cut back to the first full leaf set. Usually, it's a five-leaflet set, but some roses have seven leaflets or even more. As you deadhead, you can guide the direction of new growth by deadheading back to outward-facing (or outward-growing) buds. You will then be directing the new growth out from the center of the plant, which again is highly recommended.

COLD-HARDINESS

Roses evolved in the northern temperate areas of the world. Many Species Roses are extremely cold-hardy, surviving winters even in subarctic areas. Unfortunately, more modern rose cultivars are descended from a very small number of species, which has limited their genetic diversity, and sometimes their hardiness. Repeat-blooming hybrids are descendants of roses that originally grew in southern China. The Old Garden

One of the often overlooked English Roses, the low-growing 'Queen Nefertiti' literally covers itself with blooms.

Roses were very cold-hardy, but when they were crossed with the newly introduced China and Tea Roses in the nineteenth century, their descendants lost some of that strength.

In many of the colder areas, it is necessary to protect exposed Hybrid Tea, Floribunda, and Climbing Roses so they will survive severe winters. In some regions, this is simply a matter of mounding up leaves and straw over the rose canes to give them some protection. In the coldest zones of the country, however, it will be necessary to also mound soil over the heavily pruned canes to give them more protection. It may be more efficient, in these zones, to use Styrofoam cones or to build boxes from similar materials in order to keep the roses from freezing to death. In these coldest zones, the roses are pruned back drastically, leaving only 12 inches of cane aboveground, which then need protection.

Because of their mixed heritage, individual English Roses tolerate cold differently. Most cultivars possess reasonable winter-hardiness. Yellow roses tend to be the most tender—cultivars such as 'Graham Thomas' and 'Evelyn' will thus need to be well protected.

If you live in a cold climate, the simple answer to this issue is to be ruthless in selecting only roses that are naturally cold-tolerant. There are plenty of roses which *are* hardy, and new ones are being introduced all the time.

INSECT CONTROL

You have several choices when deciding on a strategy for insect control. Chemical insecticides have been used extensively since the end of World War II. Today we are constantly and rightly bombarded with warnings on the overuse of chemicals in the environment—remember that whatever can kill a bug has the potential to harm you. So please be aware; take precautions if you decide to use chemical insecticides.

The major insect problems for rose gardeners throughout most of this country are aphids, thrips, and Japanese beetles. Each requires a completely different approach.

APHIDS are always noted in the plural—there is no such thing as *an* aphid! And not only that, aphids are born female *and* pregnant! These are very prolific insects which sap the strength from the host plant by tapping into its cellular structure, feeding on the sap, and thereby drawing off important sugars. Colonies of aphids can be so large that their feeding will deform and weaken a plant.

Aphids are relatively easy to control. A strong spray of water will knock their very soft bodies from the plant. Simply rubbing aphids off with your hand will get rid of them as well. Try these methods before deciding on more powerful means. Like mildew, aphids are only a problem in cooler weather. The new soap-based insecticides do a good job of control and are much milder on the environment. Stronger, but with less residual toxicity are the pyrethrin-based insecticides. Originally made from the oil of chrysanthemum flowers, the pyrethrins—and the now artificially produced permethrins—give good control and are quickly broken down in the environment, posing no long-term problems.

THRIPS, also spoken of in the plural, are very small sucking insects that do most of their damage inside the buds and flowers. White and pale pink roses are the most favored hosts of thrips, and

The billowing canes of 'Peach Blossom' can be sheared back hard to create a mound of flowers.

Contrasting foliage and picturesque garden structures have been combined with 'Abraham Darby,' creating a transition from one part of the garden to the next.

the damage they cause is often seen as brown streaks and edges on the flower petals.

Thrips live inside opening rose-buds and cause damage long before the flowers are fully open. If you suspect a thrips infestation, take a plain sheet of white paper into the garden and shake a damaged bloom over the paper in the sun. If tiny, spikelike tan or black insects move about on the paper, your hunch is correct.

Highly toxic systemic insecticides, which work by being absorbed into the tissues of the plant and flowers, thereby making the whole plant toxic while providing control for thrips, are no longer recommended for indiscriminate use in the home garden. One possibility would be to treat only the infested plants with a systemic insecticide-fertilizer combination to clear up the problem. An alternative strategy is to wait for a warm, calm morning, before the wind is up, and spray either a pyrethrin-based or other similar insecticide in the air above the roses. This takes advantage of the breeding cycle of the thrips, which mate on the wing. If the damage is extensive, it will be necessary to prune off all flowers and buds, and then spray. As with any pest control, follow all label precautions.

The **JAPANESE BEETLE** is the third and, for many of us, the most difficult and voracious garden insect pest. This hard-shelled, shiny copper-green pest was inadvertently introduced from East Asia and has become a major problem for those growing roses in some parts of this

*E*nglish Roses line a path, directing the casual stroller to a restful pavilion deep in the heart of this garden.

country. The adult beetles seek out rose flowers and foliage for food and reproduction, causing extensive damage. The adult beetles do the damage, but controlling the larvae will, of course, help eradicate the problem.

Japanese beetle control is difficult at best because it takes a direct hit from any chemical assault to kill one. Hand-picking Japanese beetles off your roses and dropping them into soapy water will eliminate many of them, but others will inevitably find your roses and the problem will soon be back in force. Some growers have had luck placing pheromone traps around the garden perimeter. These hormonal scent traps attract the beetles by using their own sex chemicals to entice the male beetles to the devices. By isolating the males from the females, breeding obviously cannot take place and the life cycle is then broken.

Sex and reproduction are powerful forces, and we're quite lucky the males can't tell artificial "females" (the pheromone traps) from real ones. Be sure to place the pheromone traps away from your roses, around the farthest perimeters of your yard; otherwise, you may be calling all local beetles on the insect hotline to come visit your prize-winning English Roses!

Another defense is to use a bacterial product, available either through mail order or at your garden center, that causes death in Japanese beetle grubs. Milky spore, or *Bacillus popilliae,* attacks Japanese beetle larvae in the soil and, when used over an entire garden area, provides good protection. A combination of several or all of these strategies may be the only way to achieve control of these horrendously devastating pests.

Insect control used to be so "simple." You just went to the nursery, purchased some dreadfully toxic chemical, and nuked the garden. These days, we have to be far more aware of our actions. After all, part of our love for gardens full of beautiful flowering roses and other plants comes from our love for the environment and our planet—and our desire to preserve what we have for future generations. That puts the responsibility on us to act cautiously and wisely. Take care, take precautions, and be an aware consumer!

DISEASE CONTROL

Next to pruning, there is no area of growing that causes more concern than rose disease. Powdery mildew, black spot, and rust are a fact of rose growing in many regions of the United States. Where local conditions exist that promote problems, it will be necessary to either select resistant cultivars or take the precautions suggested below. In the worst cases, it will be necessary to live with some level of these problems since the diseases adapt faster than our ability to develop new strategies for their eradication.

POWDERY MILDEW. Commonly called mildew, powdery mildew is a silvery white, powdery fungus that grows across the surface of rose foliage and sometimes canes as well. The fungus feeds on the host plant, weakening and deforming new growth. Those parts of the country that receive summer rain and high humidity will see the problem throughout the entire growing season. In dryer regions of the West and Southwest, the season for mildew extends from first growth through to the start of real-

A WORD ABOUT SPIDER MITES

Spider mites are not insects but minute arachnid relatives of spiders that live on the underside of rose foliage. You can check for spider mites with the white paper method described for thrips. Controlling spider mites with chemicals can be researched at your local nursery, but there are two alternative methods. The first choice, again, is to select rose cultivars that have good spider mite resistance. Second, you can use a water wand with a rose-head attachment (like a showerhead) to wash off the underside of the rose foliage every one or two days until there is no more problem. It works, so be sure to try it for at least a couple of weeks before running out for any spider mite chemicals.

ly hot, dry weather, when it dies out. It then starts up again after the hot weather leaves, sometime in mid to late September. Knowing this means that if you have a problem, you will have to apply some sort of disease control during this time. The problem with the chemical controls available today is that they don't eradicate existing mildew, but only work to *prevent* infection, so these preventives must be applied *before* you see mildew.

Compared to other diseases of roses, mildew is more a cosmetic problem than a deadly one. Again the first line of defense is selecting resistant cultivars. Check the Field Guide for those cultivars with the best resistance to the problem. A number of commercial fungicides are available to prevent mildew, but less toxic strategies for mildew control are available as well. Anti-mildew soaps are somewhat effective but need regular and frequent applications and can cause damage to foliage if used too often or during very hot weather. Some growers have had success with a concoction made of one tablespoon household baking soda, one tablespoon vinegar, and one tablespoon canola oil per gallon of water used; the mixture is then sprayed as a preventive at seven- to ten-day intervals. But many growers are discovering that they can live with some mildew. This changing attitude, along with the growing availability and popularity of less toxic alternatives, is helping more and more rose lovers to regard mildew as an innocuous ailment.

BLACK SPOT. Caused by an airborne fungus that attacks rose foliage during damp and humid weather, black spot is a major disease of roses growing in regions with regular summer rain and high humidity—a severe infestation will weaken and possibly kill a rose plant. Symptoms of black spot appear on the upper leaf surface of rose foliage as circular and irregular leaf spots; the tissue surrounding the spots turns yellow, then black, and eventually the leaf drops off the bush. In extreme cases, rose canes will be infected as well.

In regions with little problem of black spot, you can pick off damaged foliage and discard it in the trash (*not* the compost). This will help keep reinfestation to a mini-

mum. In regions with severe black spot problems, the best recommendation is to first select the most resistant cultivars and then use a prophylactic spray to prevent spread of the disease. The baking soda-vinegar-oil concoction used for powdery mildew will help if you want to try less toxic alternatives. In extreme situations, consult your local garden center or agricultural advisory service before resorting to chemical controls.

RUST. Rose rust is another airborne fungus that is a problem in regions with cool temperatures and high air moisture at certain times of the year. It can be a major problem on roses grown in the western parts of the United States during the cool, moist periods of spring and fall. Symptoms first appear as rusty red to orange spots on the underside of foliage. Later, rusty spots will appear on the upper surfaces. In late summer, black pustules are often produced, which carry the disease through the winter.

Rose rust can be a major problem in regions with optimal conditions for the spread of the disease—the selection of resistant cultivars can't be overemphasized. Picking off infested foliage and discarding it in the trash will help in minor infections, but honestly, this can be a grueling, ongoing ordeal. Chemical alternatives will be needed in the worst cases, but it's in everyone's best interest to make cultivar choices that will make them unnecessary. Many of the same chemical prophylactics used for controlling powdery mildew and black spot will also help control rose rust.

A Simple, Step-by-Step System for Healthy Roses

To correct problems, we Westerners tend to work backward from symptoms to develop approaches to alleviate those symptoms rather than approaches geared to discovering and correcting underlying causes. For some time now, a number of growers have refused to go along with this trend, which in rose gardening means emphasizing problems over horticulture. One of the difficulties in getting people to plant roses in the landscape is this focus on the inconvenience. Everyone believes that roses are difficult plants, far too susceptible to disease to be worth the trouble. Of course, there can be problems growing healthy roses, but the problems should not be, and do not need to be, the main focus. We grow roses for the joy they bring into our lives; for their beauty, their perfume, and for the aesthetic glow they impart to the garden. These qualities alone are enough to greatly outweigh any hardships of maintenance.

Most rose problems are more a matter of cosmetics than anything else. Develop an informed, realistic approach to gardening. How many aphids can you live with? How much mildew on your prize red rose will you tolerate before you are forced to resort to active prevention? Rosarians are discovering they can live with quite a lot of "natural cosmetic interferences" and still have healthy roses. Discover for yourself how much of any problem your garden can handle before you need to take action.

1. Select problem-resistant cultivars appropriate for your garden and area.

This is a gardener's first line of defense. Select healthy cultivars and *prune with a shovel* any plants that are too prone to problems. Be ruthless! Network with friends and other gardeners in your area to identify specific cultivars with strong natural resistance to the problems you can expect to face in your garden. Visit local display gardens and make notes of healthy cultivars. Cultivate a relationship with a reliable local retail nursery for dependable information. And finally, don't believe everything the catalogs say. Educate yourself.

2. Improve or change your horticultural practices with a view to growing healthier plants.

Healthy plants are more resistant to common rose problems. Stress opens the door for disease and pests, so avoid putting the garden under stress. Space plants so they receive adequate sun and air circulation. Mulch the beds to keep down competition from weeds and to help keep roots cool and moist. If possible, keep water off foliage late in the day or, if you must water overhead, irrigate early in the day so that the foliage has time to dry before the sun goes down.

3. Employ nontoxic mechanical or manual pest controls.

Pick aphids off by hand or flush them off with a strong stream of water. A number of traps are now available for whiteflies, ants, beetles, and snails. Snails, slugs, and large grasshoppers can be dispatched without resorting to chemical sprays—step on them. Pick off foliage infected with fungal problems like black spot and rust. This will help keep the fungus from spreading to noninfected plants.

4. Practice biological warfare.

Encourage the natural systems already in our environment to help keep problems in check. Realize that the birds and beneficial insects in your garden are also affected by chemical insecticides, so to keep a more natural balance in your domain, select interventions that take the total system into account. Look into beneficial insects such as ladybug, lacewing, and praying mantis garden kits. Release these predatory insects (available at nurseries and through mail order) into your garden and let them do the work for you. If you have ducks, allow them to roam through the garden to pick off one of their favorite delicacies, snails. In some parts of the country, you can release predators known as Decollate snails, which will help bring your local onslaught of the larger, common brown snail under complete control over time. There are also new products, made from natural plant sources, that can be used in place of artificial chemicals to slow the spread of some attackers. By developing a relationship with your local nursery personnel, you'll be able to keep tabs on new advancements in the future as well.

5. Resort to chemicals only after all other methods have been tried.

For some, this will be the most controversial step; chemicals are their long-cherished crutch. Many other gardeners have made a conscious decision not to use any chemicals at all. Whatever side of the fence you're on, it's always best to start with the least toxic approach, such as insecticidal soaps, dormant oils, and the like. Second choice would be short-lived pesticides like pyrethrins. And finally, when specific problems are completely out of hand, look for specific chemical controls and apply only to the affected plants; *don't* spray the whole garden when only one or two plants are infested. In each case, use these products with the utmost care.

Rose care can be as complex or simple as the individual gardener wishes to make it. For some, following a well-defined set of rules gives a sense of security; for others, learning by experience promotes a feeling of excitement and discovery. No matter what method works for you, learn by observing your garden. When deadheading, look at the way each individual cultivar has responded to your care. Does a rose exhibit signs of distress or is it thriving, free of insects and disease? How did it respond to your pruning technique? Does it produce flowers on a regular schedule, as it should?

Keeping a garden journal or marking a calendar can be a source of important information for the next season. For me, simplicity is best. But always remember your horticultural roots. Good horticulture is good husbandry. Your garden will tell you when it is healthy and happy. Watch it, and listen to it!

A KEY *to the* FIELD GUIDE

P hotographs of all cultivars in the Field Guide were taken in the spring and early summer of 1996 in the gardens of The Huntington Library, Art Collections, and Botanical Gardens, located in San Marino, California; Descanso Gardens, located in La Cañada-Flintridge, California; and Heirloom Old Garden Roses, located in St. Paul, Oregon.

Rose cultivars are listed alphabetically. The **CULTIVAR NAME** appears as the title, followed by the **YEAR OF INTRODUCTION** (the year the cultivar was first offered for sale).

HYBRIDIZER lists the name of the person who produced the cultivar.

SUITABILITY indicates just how easy or difficult a cultivar is to grow.

AVAILABILITY lists the best information known regarding consumer access. **WIDE** indicates a rose that should be easy to find; **MAIL-ORDER** cultivars are those listed in a variety of catalogs; and **LIMITED** denotes a rose available through catalogs listed in Appendix A.

STATURE & HABIT indicates the size to which a particular cultivar will grow in both **WARM** and **COOL** climates.

FRAGRANCE describes the flower's scent.

USES gives a few of the primary uses for each cultivar.

PARENTAGE is listed where that information is available. The female (or seed) parent is always listed first and the male (or pollen) parent is listed second.

DISEASES mentions problems you need to look out for, because the cultivar is particularly susceptible to them.

DENOMINATION lists the internationally accepted code name, used throughout the rose world. The first three letters indicate the hybridizer.

PATENTS are listed for those cultivars that have been so protected. Plant patents are issued to hybridizers and/or their agents and currently, in the United States, are good for 17 years.

ABRAHAM DARBY

[*1985*]

Readily available and widely grown, 'Abraham Darby' earns high praise with strong, robust growth; healthy, disease-resistant foliage; overpowering fragrance; and power of rebloom. This popular rose can be grown as a freestanding shrub or, in the right climate zone, as a small climber of up to 10 feet. Cold-hardiness may be a problem in more northern regions, so take appropriate precautions.

Flowers begin as large, fat yellow buds that progress to classically shaped, shallow-cupped blooms in clusters of three to five. Fully open, the flowers can span from 4 to 5 inches across, and they hold the shallow-cupped formation throughout their lives. Flowers can be soft pink with apricot tones in cool seasons and progress to a peachy apricot blend with yellow and cream tones at other times. The fragrance is strong and fruity. The plant covers itself with healthy, large, leathery, deep green foliage and plentiful, large red prickles. Some rust has been observed on this cultivar, so be forewarned if this tends to be a problem in your area. 'Abraham Darby' also tends to hold on to his deadheads, so you'll need to monitor the plant to keep it looking fresh and clean. Blooms are produced throughout the growing season with wanton regularity, and they hold well as cut flowers. Sunlight works wonders with this rose, casting playful shadows and highlights across its fully petaled flowers.

In warmer areas of the country, this cultivar will grow to 6 feet high and achieve an equal spread. If this is a bit too large for your garden, try self-pegging—it works.

'Abraham Darby' commemorates an eighteenth-century Quaker and iron master, one of the founders of the Industrial Revolution.

HYBRIDIZER: David Austin
SUITABILITY: all levels
AVAILABILITY: wide
STATURE & HABIT: 6 to 8 feet × 6 feet (warm climate); 5 feet × 4 feet (cool climate)
FRAGRANCE: strong and fruity

USES: tall shrub, climber, cutting
PARENTAGE: 'Yellow Cushion' × 'Aloha'
DISEASE: rust
DENOMINATION: AUScot
PATENT: 7215

Abraham Darby

ADMIRED MIRANDA

[*1983*]

It is difficult not to admire this Miranda, another Austin rose with a delicious fragrance, blended with perfection in old-fashioned-style blooms. This is not, however, a rose for the beginner. She will take several years to settle into a garden and produce her best flowers, but if you are up to a challenge and love the color and fragrance, she might be the rose to try after you've cut your teeth on some of the easier varieties.

'Admired Miranda' is definitely among the lowest of the low-growing Austins; she can take quite some time to build up to 2 feet in height. Flowers are produced in clusters of round yellow-orange buds that open to quartered, flat, rosette-shaped blooms some 3 to 3½ inches across in warm apricot-pink tones. Repeat bloom is quite good, and the fragrance is strong and fruity. New growth is red-bronze with bright red prickles. Foliage is a shiny dark green and covers the plant well but is subject to all the problems that come with mildew, rust, and black spot.

Some roses can take a while to fully settle into their environment, so it's always best to give a new cultivar three years to prove itself, and 'Admired Miranda' is a good example of the need for patience. During the first few years, the plant growth is open and somewhat angular, but as it matures it does begin to fill out. This rose grows well in a container, where you can give her all the tender loving care she craves. Another option would be to plant three bushes in tight formation, a cluster with plants no more than 1½ feet apart, so that the canes will grow to interlock, producing a low mound of color at the front of your border.

'Admired Miranda' is named for Prospero's daughter in Shakespeare's *The Tempest*.

HYBRIDIZER: David Austin
SUITABILITY: advanced
AVAILABILITY: mail order
STATURE & HABIT: 2 feet × 2 feet (warm climate); 4 feet × 3 feet (cool climate)
FRAGRANCE: strong, fruity

USES: border, bedding, container
PARENTAGE: 'The Friar' × 'The Friar'
DISEASES: mildew, rust, black spot
DENOMINATION: AUSrush

*Admired
Miranda*

AMBRIDGE ROSE

[*1990*]

From the very first bloom, 'Ambridge Rose' was a knockout. I planted five bushes at a focal point at the end of a bed a few years ago, and to this day the display is all any gardener could desire.

Flowers are produced from clusters of round buds that open into blooms 3 to 3½ inches across. The deep-cupped flowers are peachy apricot with pale pink scalloped and ruffled outer petals that fade to almost white—not at all an unattractive metamorphosis. The fragrance is strong myrrh with a pleasing fruity undertone. The new growth is bronze. This rose seems never to be out of bloom, with new buds constantly replacing spent flowers. Flower petals drop cleanly, a trait appreciated by all of us who don't get out into the garden to do our daily deadheading. The low-growing plant covers itself with dark green foliage and well-spaced red prickles.

Apricot is not a color usually associated with Old Garden Roses (OGRs), but the flower formation of 'Ambridge Rose,' with its deeply cupped blooms and reflexed outer petals, harks back to the classic Gallicas grown at Empress Josephine's gardens at Château Malmaison. Disease need not be a major concern for 'Ambridge Rose' growers. Most apricot and yellow roses are less cold-hardy and often do not fare well in the coldest zones. On the other hand, roses of these colors fade in the hottest sun of the warm zones, where a bit of shade might help preserve their delicate tones. With minor protection, this rose should grow in most areas of the country, cool zones included. Austin lists the parentage as 'Charles Austin' crossed by a seedling that could have been 'Wife of Bath.' This cultivar produces armloads of flowers for cutting and is proving to be almost as popular as the other great apricot English Rose, 'Tamora.' With minimal extra care, 'Ambridge Rose' is recommended for all zones and is particularly suited to the warm to hot climate regions.

The name commemorates a long-running BBC serial, *The Archers,* which takes place in the fictional village of Ambridge.

HYBRIDIZER: David Austin
SUITABILITY: all levels
AVAILABILITY: limited
STATURE & HABIT: 3 feet ×
  2½ feet (warm climate);
  2 feet × 2½ feet (cool climate)
FRAGRANCE: strong myrrh, fruity

USES: border, low hedge,
  bedding, cutting
PARENTAGE: 'Charles Austin' ×
  seedling
DISEASE: slight mildew
DENOMINATION: AUSwonder
PATENT: 8679

*Ambridge
Rose*

BELLE STORY

[*1984*]

This dainty, low-growing rose is flushed with sweet charm and alluring individuality. It would be difficult to live without 'Belle Story'; I try to include at least one or two in any garden I plant. Like many of Austin's best English Roses, 'Belle Story' has the great landscape Shrub Rose 'Iceberg' as one of its parents. 'Iceberg' seems to have the ability to impart its grace as a landscape shrub, as well as the charm of its flower, to its descendants.

'Belle Story' covers itself with large, dark green foliage having good natural disease-resistance. The plant can grow to 3 or 4 feet tall and will be a bit wider than tall. This is one of those cultivars that works best when grouped in plantings of three or more for maximum effect. The flowers are shallow-cupped. They open from pointed buds to semi-double blooms of pale peachy pink with a hint of yellow at the petal base, and display red-gold stamens at the center. The outer guard petals reflex back, giving the flat, open flowers a grace and charm equaled only by the classic OGRs. An outstanding cultivar, it is almost always in continuous bloom and the flowers have a wonderfully strong fragrance of myrrh with a spicy overtone. Flowers can be as large as 4½ inches across with the center bud opening to a 6-inch spread.

This cultivar commemorates the first woman to serve in the Royal Navy as a nursing sister in the 1880s. Belle was one of just a few women who actually served shipboard at a time when the navy was not considered a fit place for a woman. Like her namesake, this rose is a tough lady who will charm your socks off.

HYBRIDIZER: David Austin
SUITABILITY: all levels
AVAILABILITY: wide
STATURE & HABIT: 4 feet ×
 4 feet (warm climate);
 4 feet × 4 feet (cool climate)
FRAGRANCE: strong myrrh and
 spicy

USES: border, low hedge,
 container, cutting, partial
 shade
PARENTAGE: ('Chaucer' ×
 'Parade') × ('The Prioress' ×
 'Iceberg')
DISEASES: slight mildew, rust
DENOMINATION: AUSelle

Belle Story

BIBI MAIZOON

[*1989*]

To date, this has not been an easy rose for me to grow. It could be that it's one of those plants that takes a few years to settle into a garden. Compact, low growing, and somewhat weak, my original specimen was defoliated by rust. But happily, my four newer plants are proving to have the hardiness and growth power that are described in the catalogs.

Round pink buds with lighter edges open to 2½-inch, deeply cupped flowers that retain the cup shape throughout their bloom. The flowers are warm pink and have a strong rose and fruity fragrance. The foliage starts out with a decidedly reddish tint, and the smooth, almost thornless light green canes mature to light green with reddish prickles. The canes have a distinctive zigzag growth habit. Austin speaks of this cultivar's having large, Centifolia-like flowers. To this point, the plants have produced infrequent flowerings with rather weak stems that can't quite hold up the large blossoms, and so they tend to droop. This will probably improve with age as the bush develops strength. Leaves are made up of seven leaflets.

Disease can be a problem with this cultivar, but with some protection and extra care, the shrub will overcome most attackers. All things considered, 'Bibi Maizoon' will make a lovely low hedge.

The right to name this cultivar was purchased by a private party in the United Kingdom; the name is that of a family member. You might have seen this rose spelled 'Bibi Mezoon,' but Austin later corrected it to the current form.

HYBRIDIZER: David Austin
SUITABILITY: connoisseur
AVAILABILITY: wide
STATURE & HABIT: 2 feet ×
   2 feet (warm climate);
   4 feet × 4 feet (cool climate)
FRAGRANCE: sweetly fragrant

USES: border, low hedge,
   container
PARENTAGE: 'The Reeve' ×
   'Chaucer'
DISEASES: mildew, rust,
   black spot
DENOMINATION: AUSdimindo
PATENT: 8092

Bibi Maizoon

BOW BELLS

[*1991*]

The blooms of 'Bow Bells' bear a strong resemblance to those of the Bourbon Rose 'Reine Victoria'; otherwise, there is a distinct appearance of the Modern Shrub Rose to the bush. If left unpruned, it can grow to 6 feet or more, but the flowers suffer as the plant gets too tall.

Flowers are produced in large sprays of three to five buds that are long, pointed, and red. Cupped blooms are 3½ inches across, of a most luminous, strong, and lush pink with prominent gold stamens for the viewing—if you look over the bowing inner petals. The fragrance is mild with a sweet, rosy cast. Medium green foliage blankets the plant. Allowed to grow to its full 6- or 8-foot height, it will tend to stay upright until flower buds form; then the long, thin canes get heavy and flop over. 'Bow Bells' may do better with some protection from intense sun to help retain its color and flower size. This bush may take a while to settle into the garden, but once it does, flowers are produced with Floribunda-like regularity, and rebloom is admirable.

Although you may notice some mildew, that doesn't seem to be much of a problem and it won't interfere with the bloom cycle. You will need to deadhead this rose regularly; if not, new growth will surround the old deadheads and continue to grow and flower, giving the plant a rather untidy appearance. Understand, however, that you will be greatly rewarded for your extra effort. The unusual bell-shaped flowers are quite alluring and make 'Bow Bells' a very interesting addition to any garden.

Christopher Wren, the renowned seventeenth-century English architect, built fifty-two of London's most beautiful churches, one of which was St. Mary-le-Bow in the Cheapside district. It used to be said that anyone claiming to be a true Cockney had to have been born within hearing distance of the "Bow bells."

HYBRIDIZER: David Austin
SUITABILITY: all levels
AVAILABILITY: mail order
STATURE & HABIT: 6 feet × 4 feet (warm climate); 4 feet × 3 feet (cool climate)
FRAGRANCE: mild, sweet rose

USES: border, low hedge, container, partial shade
PARENTAGE: ('Chaucer' × 'Conrad Ferdinand Meyer') × 'Graham Thomas'
DISEASES: mild mildew, black spot
DENOMINATION: AUSbells

Bow Bells

BREDON

[*1984*]

A lthough the flowers of this cultivar have that English Rose appearance, the plant itself is very modern, with a Floribunda-like growth habit. The shrub does grow a bit tall for a low-growing English Rose, but there is room for differences in the group and the garden.

'Bredon' (pronounced BREE-dun) cloaks itself with shiny dark green foliage and numerous sharp red prickles. The small, rosette-shaped flowers are 3 inches across and are produced in large sprays with as many as fifteen buds in a cluster. Buds are greenish white to start with, opening to creamy white with a bit of yellow and soft peach tones at the center. This cultivar repeats well and has a mild, sweet fragrance. New growth is edged red and the dark green foliage often has seven leaflets.

This rose does have a few faults. It has a tendency to mildew, especially on the peduncles just below the buds; and it holds on to its deadheads, which must be removed manually to promote reblooming. This is another English Rose whose deadheading must be done faithfully; otherwise, its faded blooms will give the plant the overall look of discarded brown tissue paper. For a stronger statement, try planting this cultivar in groups of three.

The name commemorates Bredon Hill, a site near the Austin nursery in Hereford and Worcester, which is referred to in "To an Athlete Dying Young," a poem by A. E. Housman.

HYBRIDIZER: David Austin
SUITABILITY: all levels
AVAILABILITY: wide
STATURE & HABIT: 4 feet ×
  2 feet (warm climate);
  3 feet × 5 feet (cool climate)
FRAGRANCE: light rose

USES: border, low hedge,
  container, partial shade
PARENTAGE: 'Wife of Bath' ×
  'Lilian Austin'
DISEASES: mildew, rust
DENOMINATION: AUSbred

Bredon

BROTHER CADFAEL

[*1990*]

Need a tall rose for the back of the border? This one can be a great addition to any garden with some space and height to fill up. A prime English Rose for self-pegging, the long, supple canes are almost thornless. Try arching 'Brother Cadfael' over a wall or fence, as he really wants to climb.

The flowers are very large, often as much as 5 inches across, globular, and very full. Blooms start out a lovely soft pink color and are ruffled on the edges with the outer petals reflexing downward. They are very fragrant with a strong rose and fruit perfume. So far, this has proved to be a shy bloomer, although rebloom can be improved by pegging. The dark green foliage contrasts well with the flowers. New canes are a lovely bronze-red and grow long very quickly. 'Brother Cadfael' does occasionally attract some mildew, but he doesn't seem to present too much of a problem. To produce very large flowers like this, the plant has to expend a lot of food and energy, so it may take a bit more time between cycles for the plant to build up its strength and produce blooms again.

This cultivar is named for the medieval monk-detective in Ellis Peters's mystery novels. Her Brother Cadfael is an herbalist and sleuth who uses his rather un-brotherly worldly talents to solve the occasional murder in the monastery.

HYBRIDIZER: David Austin
SUITABILITY: all levels
AVAILABILITY: mail order
STATURE & HABIT: 8 feet ×
  5 feet (warm climate);
  4 feet × 3 feet (cool climate)
FRAGRANCE: strong rose with a
  fruity cast

USES: tall shrub, back of
  border, self-pegging, low
  climber, cutting
PARENTAGE: 'Charles Austin' ×
  seedling
DISEASE: mildew
DENOMINATION: AUSglobe
PATENT: 8681

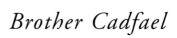

Brother Cadfael

CANTERBURY

[*1969*]

Canterbury is one of the earliest of Austin's introductions. Classed as a single-petaled flower, it often does have more than one row of petals, but the overall look is still that of a single rose. The flowers are so large that at first the stems can't hold them up. And it is only after a few years' growth that the plant builds up its strength and produces enough flowers to justify garden space. A weak grower, this cultivar will take some patience and a few years to establish itself.

Blooms come from long, pointed buds that open to rosy pink, semi-double flowers as large as 6 inches across. The fully open flowers display a hint of yellow at the base and have lovely gold stamens. The fragrance is only mild at best. The shrub is open and lax, needing some support at first from those useful green garden stakes and ties, at least until it has a few years' growth under its belt. Cut flowers hold well, although they are at their best when picked just as the bud is starting to unfurl. The dark green foliage has reasonable resistance to disease. Austin seems to feel that this shrub does not have a lot of vigor, but it does do well in the United States. In more northern and temperate zones, it is described as a small, spreading shrub.

'Canterbury' is named for the city in eastern Kent, England, and for the eleventh-century cathedral built there. Thomas Becket was martyred at the site in 1170, and it was the destination of the travelers in Chaucer's *The Canterbury Tales.*

HYBRIDIZER: David Austin
SUITABILITY: all levels
AVAILABILITY: mail order
STATURE & HABIT: 5 feet ×
   5 feet (warm climate); 2½ feet
   × 2½ feet (cool climate)
FRAGRANCE: mild

USES: bedding, cutting
PARENTAGE: ('Monique' ×
   'Constance Spry') × seedling
DISEASES: mildew, rust
DENOMINATION: none

Canterbury

CARDINAL HUME

[*1984*]

Technically not an English Rose, 'Cardinal Hume' is often included with this class because it has so many similarities. Its complex parentage really sets it off from the usual run of garden roses, as does the unique color of the flowers. The plant has proved to be rather difficult to place in most gardens as its growth habit is much wider than it is tall. One friend trained this rose to grow into a low fruit tree, which is an ingenious solution, but 'Cardinal Hume' isn't really a climber. My ultimate solution was to train the canes up and around a tripod made of three green garden stakes. In this way, a rather unruly shrub was brought under control.

The plant makes long spreading canes with flowers produced in large terminal clusters—upwards of twenty to thirty buds in a cluster have been counted at the height of bloom. Flowers are individually 2½ inches across, deep red-purple, and mildly fragrant. The petals have a distinctive pointed tip and are folded on the outer edge, which gives the flowers a star-shape outline; many of the small center petaloids have white quills. New growth is reddish and smooth and the foliage is dark green and large, with seven leaflets that cover the plant well. New canes are produced at an unusual 45 degree angle from the main canes. 'Cardinal Hume' produces a fine crop of small round hips in the fall. Disease problems are nonexistent.

The color, very reminiscent of dark purple Gallicas, is not found in too many Modern Roses, and in my opinion, one needs to be somewhat circumspect when using this rose in the garden. The developer, Harkness & Co., Ltd., also introduced a fragrant sister seedling from the same parentage in 1987, called 'Rochester Cathedral.' The color is pink-purple with silver reverse. Although 'Rochester Cathedral' is not commonly grown in the United States, its color would work somewhat better in our gardens.

This cultivar is named for G. Basil Hume, the Roman Catholic Archbishop of Westminster, who became a cardinal in 1976.

HYBRIDIZER: Harkness
SUITABILITY: all levels
AVAILABILITY: mail order
STATURE & HABIT: 6 feet × 8 feet (warm climate); 3 feet × 3½ feet (cool climate)
FRAGRANCE: mild
USES: bedding, low climber, pegging
PARENTAGE: (seedling × ['Orange Sensation' × 'Allgold'] × *Rosa californica*) × 'Frank Naylor'
DISEASE: none
DENOMINATION: HARregale

Cardinal Hume

CHARLES AUSTIN

[*1973*]

Among the first Austin roses I planted back in 1986, this culti-var was my introduction to the burdensome absence of accu-rate information on how these roses grow in the United States. I planted a selection of English Roses that had been growing in con-tainers, using descriptions from the Austin catalog. The information on 'Charles Austin' specified a maximum height of 2 to 3 feet. From March to August, this cultivar—planted, of course, at the front of the bed— grew to more than 10 feet tall! Charles has long since been relocated to a more appropriate place at the center of a large bed.

Large orangish yellow buds produce lightly fragrant flowers that can be as much as 4 inches across and full of warm apricot petals with just a hint of yellow at the center, fading to buff pink. Blooms are usu-ally produced in small clusters of three. Large, oval, medium green foliage is contrasted by large red prickles. Fragrance is light. Some mildew is found on this rose from time to time, but disease is not much of a problem overall.

Hard pruning seems to suit this rose just fine. After each flower-ing cycle, you can prune back hard to encourage rebloom. Like so many of the tall-growing Austin roses, Charles blooms only at the ends of the long canes when growing upright, which makes this shrub a great can-didate for self-pegging.

Named for the hybridizer's father, this cultivar seems to be hardy in most U.S. climate zones.

HYBRIDIZER: David Austin

SUITABILITY: all levels

AVAILABILITY: mail order

STATURE & HABIT: 10 feet, but can be kept to 5 feet × 6 feet (warm climate); 5 feet × 4 feet (cool climate)

FRAGRANCE: light

USES: bedding, climber, pegging, cutting

PARENTAGE: 'Aloha' × 'Chaucer'

DISEASES: slight mildew, black spot

DENOMINATION: none

Charles Austin

CHARLES RENNIE MACKINTOSH

[*1988*]

Pinky lilac is not my favorite flower color. This bush, however, does have a certain distinctive charm. And it is one of those roses that blooms in the heat of August. There are lots of roses that like the cool of spring, but there are not many that go into overdrive, flowerwise, in the sweltering heat of midsummer!

Loads of fat reddish pink buds open to pink-lilac flowers with a tinge of gray. Flowers are shallow cups, 3 inches across and full of scalloped petals. The outer guard petals reflex back much like one of the parents, 'Mary Rose.' The foliage is light green and somewhat small but does cover the plant well with shiny oval leaflets. Spring foliage can be spotted by mildew, but with the advent of hot weather, that becomes much less of a problem. Growth is on the twiggy side, but both the initial spring bloom and the repeat bloom improve with each passing year.

I would not have given 'Charles Rennie Mackintosh' much attention—I guess I am prejudiced against lavender—except that a friend and volunteer forced me to accept the virtues of this cultivar. The light green foliage seems to have an almost gray cast and is a perfect foil for the flowers. It is the frequency of repeat bloom, though, that never fails to amaze me.

This rose was named for a prominent Scottish architect, painter, and designer who died in 1928.

HYBRIDIZER: David Austin
SUITABILITY: all levels
AVAILABILITY: mail order
STATURE & HABIT: 5 feet ×
4 feet (warm climate); 3 feet ×
2½ feet (cool climate)
FRAGRANCE: mild

USES: bedding, border, cutting
PARENTAGE: ('Chaucer' ×
'Conrad Ferdinand Meyer') ×
'Mary Rose'
DISEASES: mildew, black spot
DENOMINATION: AUSren
PATENT: 8155

Charles Rennie Mackintosh

CHARLOTTE

[*1993*]

I t is truly a shame that this rose isn't more available. A new introduction from the Austin nursery, you will just have to wait until someone in the United States puts her on the market. I have been growing 'Charlotte' for the past year and have fallen in love with her. She is a tall grower, but a light pruning between flowering cycles will keep her in bounds for most gardens.

Flowers are so deeply cupped, they are globular. Pointed yellow buds open to 3½ inches across and are a pure, soft, buttery yellow. The outer petals fade to almost white, while the centers remain lemon yellow. New growth is a light green edged with bronze with an occasional red prickle. Foliage is light green, and the five- to seven-leaflet leaves are large and cover the plant well. The fragrance reminds me of Tea Roses with a sweet, fruity aftertaste.

All in all, there is a certain charm and grace to this plant and flower. Repeat bloom is good and consistent. Having 'Graham Thomas' as one of its parents can't hurt this rose, but it does seem to be a somewhat smaller grower. With some judicious pruning during the growing season, this shrub, which can reach 5 feet or so, can be kept to 3 feet. The color of this rose does hold up better with some protection from the hottest sun.

HYBRIDIZER: David Austin
SUITABILITY: all levels
AVAILABILITY: limited
STATURE & HABIT: 5 feet ×
   4 feet (warm climate);
   3 feet × 2½ feet (cool
   climate)
FRAGRANCE: Tea-like and fruity

USES: bedding, border, cutting
PARENTAGE: ('Chaucer' ×
   'Conrad Ferdinand Meyer') ×
   'Graham Thomas'
DISEASES: mildew, black spot
DENOMINATION: AUSpoly
PATENT: 9008

Charlotte

CHARMIAN

[*1982*]

O f all the English Roses, this one comes the closest to being a true climber; also, it is one of the most fragrant of the group. If left on its own, 'Charmian' will make a large, floppy shrub that will need some sort of support. One of the nice things about this cultivar is that it is so amenable to training, pruned hard as a shrub, or onto a support, or over a wall as a climber.

A hardy shrub, 'Charmian' has large, dark green foliage, often with seven leaflets, which creates a wonderful background for the blossoms. Flowers are produced in large terminal clusters of twenty or more fat round buds. These are followed by 3-inch deep pink flowers that open flat with a wonderful, heady, Old Rose fragrance. If trained horizontally, the bush can be encouraged to break along the canes, which will improve the repeat bloom of this cultivar. New growth is light green edged with bronze.

Give this rose the room it's going to need. Try training it up into a low-growing fruit tree, or as a low climber spilling over a wall. When pruned back hard, it has prodigious terminal clusters with unbelievable trusses of bloom. Training works for this rose and, no matter what, her soft charm comes through to warm the heart.

Charmian was Cleopatra's faithful attendant in *Antony and Cleopatra*. After Cleopatra's death, Charmian applies the asp to her own breast just as Octavius's guards enter the tomb.

HYBRIDIZER: David Austin
SUITABILITY: all levels
AVAILABILITY: mail order
STATURE & HABIT: 8 feet ×
  6 feet (warm climate);
  3½ feet × 3½ feet (cool
  climate)
FRAGRANCE: strong Old Rose

USES: border, climber, cutting
PARENTAGE: 'Lilian Austin' ×
  seedling
DISEASES: mildew, black spot
DENOMINATION: AUSmian

Charmian

CHAUCER

[*1970*]

Without fail, every time visitors walk around my garden, they stop to take a long look at this cultivar. The first impression is invariably made by the glorious, pale pink flowers; the second by the fragrance, which is overwhelming; and the third by all the mildew! This rose has a strong dose of Old Rose in him, and it shows. Large, crisp blooms are highly evocative of the classic Gallicas of yore, and as such the flower would not look out of place in Empress Josephine's garden. The flowers do bear a strong resemblance to its Gallica parent, 'Duchesse de Montebello.'

This compact-growing bush produces flowers that are a large 4½ inches across, deeply cupped, soft blush pink with a button eye, and very fragrant. Foliage is medium green, large, and *very* prone to mildew. The perfume is unique, described by Austin and others as reminiscent of myrrh. The plant is strong and upright, often producing flowers in clusters of six or so globular buds. Repeat bloom is excellent. New growth is bronze, and the prickles are red with green tips.

Don't let the mildew stop you. It hasn't stopped me or my friends from growing this lovely rose. If you are looking for a repeat-blooming rose with the grace and flowers typical of the old Dutch Masters, this rose is for you. Cut early, in the half-open bud stage, the flowers will hold well, and the perfume is unbelievable. Plant 'Chaucer' in groups of three or use him as an accent plant in the border mixed with herbs and perennials for maximum effect.

This cultivar was named for Geoffrey Chaucer, the English poet and author of *The Canterbury Tales.*

HYBRIDIZER: David Austin
SUITABILITY: all levels
AVAILABILITY: mail order
STATURE & HABIT: 4 feet ×
  3 feet (warm climate);
  3½ feet × 3 feet (cool
  climate)
FRAGRANCE: strong myrrh

USES: border, container,
  cutting
PARENTAGE: 'Duchesse de
  Montebello' × 'Constance
  Spry'
DISEASES: mildew, rust
DENOMINATION: none

Chaucer

CHIANTI

[*1967*]

Tall, lusty shrubs that bloom only once in the spring are not much in favor now, but my suggestion is that if you have the room, either amid the shrubbery or at the back of a border, you might try this one. The great Old Gallica Rose 'Tuscany' is one of its parents; thus the once-blooming characteristic. Except for its size, which is tall, this is one of the most Old Rose-looking of the English Roses. Thin canes well covered with mean prickles of varying sizes, as well as the foliage and flower, all point to its Gallica heritage.

This is definitively a tall shrub, the growth of which is rather lax and arching, so give it all the room it needs. Fat, round red buds produce large flowers 3 inches across, cupped and colored a deep crimson that ages purplish maroon. 'Chianti' is very fragrant with the wonderful, classic Old Rose scents that invariably seem to bring fond memories of a grandparent's roses. The long thin canes are well covered with prickles, and dark green foliage grows in seven leaflets with the tip leaflet often pointing downward. Even though large, this cultivar has a truly Old Rose charm and should not be overlooked where the space is available.

From 'Chianti' were produced both 'The Knight' and 'The Squire,' the two cultivars from which all the red Austin roses descend, even the modern-appearing 'L. D. Braithwaite.' The search for the perfect red rose goes on, but these are all admirable candidates. The large size and lack of repeat bloom may prevent some of us from growing 'Chianti,' but it is truly one of Austin's best. I like it for more than just its atavistic charms, although they do have great appeal. Those of you in cold climate zones should love it for its cold-hardiness.

This cultivar is named for the dry red wine produced in the Monte Chianti region of Tuscany. Note how the name reflects its parentage.

HYBRIDIZER: David Austin
SUITABILITY: all levels
AVAILABILITY: mail order
STATURE & HABIT: 8 feet ×
   8 feet (warm climate);
   5 feet × 5 feet (cool climate)
FRAGRANCE: strong Old Rose

USES: mixed border, tall hedge
PARENTAGE: 'Dusky Maiden' ×
   'Tuscany'
DISEASE: mildew
DENOMINATION: none

Chianti

CLAIRE ROSE

[*1986*]

The flowers of 'Claire Rose' are displayed to perfection against the dark green foliage, but at times it can be a most perplexing garden shrub. This is a super rose but it does grow tall, and there seems to be a problem getting it to rebloom after a hard pruning—it appears to need to grow tall again before reblooming. Other growers, however, have not complained of this problem, so it may just be a matter of placement. The flower form and color remind me of the great Old Bourbon 'Souvenir de la Malmaison.'

The fat pink buds open to large, 4-inch flowers in very full but shallow cups; these flatten out to quartered, soft pink blooms that are deeper-colored at the center and fade to blush white on the outer edges. The flowers have a strong, Tea-like fragrance and are often produced in clusters of three or four per stem. The perfection of the bloom must be seen to be believed—nothing else comes close to it—and the flower petals have so much substance that they hold both on the bush and as cut flowers. Rain can cause the petals to spot, which is not an uncommon problem with lighter-colored roses. The foliage is dark green with seven leaflets.

'Claire Rose' is quite amenable to training; the shrub is probably at its best either pegged or trained over a fence as a climber. My plant has been so heavy with bloom that it had to be propped up with garden stakes to keep it from collapsing. If you don't have room for a shrub this size, try either self-pegging or hard pruning to keep it in shape.

Another rose named for Austin's family, this time a daughter.

HYBRIDIZER: David Austin
SUITABILITY: all levels
AVAILABILITY: mail order
STATURE & HABIT: 8 feet ×
    4 feet (warm climate);
    4 feet × 3 feet (cool climate)
FRAGRANCE: sweet and Tea-like

USES: tall shrub, cutting, partial shade
PARENTAGE: 'Charles Austin' ×
    (seedling × 'Iceberg')
DISEASE: slight mildew
DENOMINATION: AUSlight

Claire
Rose

CONSTANCE SPRY

[*1961*]

The first English Rose and the one to set the standard for all that come after. She may have been the original, but she is still one of the most loved of Austin's introductions. A tall grower, this once-bloomer is definitely not for the small garden or faint of heart. Constance is best kept as a large freestanding shrub or trained as a climber. The term "hybrid vigor" was used in the nineteenth century to describe roses that exhibited stronger growth and energy than either of its parents, and 'Constance Spry' has lots of hybrid vigor.

Fat, round pink buds, yellow at the base, open to 4-inch, deeply cupped, warm pink flowers that possess a heavenly sweet fragrance. New growth is long and thin with bronze tones. The foliage is a dark green, which contrasts beautifully with the red prickles. Leaves are folded along their center rib and the end leaflet bends downward.

This cultivar doesn't seem to bloom quite as well in our warmer climates as it does in the colder parts of the country. Anyone who has seen the photograph of 'Constance Spry' in bloom on the wall at Mottisfont Abbey will want it. Be forewarned, though, this is a big, lusty shrub that takes room to grow and can be a shy bloomer as well.

Constance Spry (1886–1960) was an English gardener, flower arranger, and author of *Flower Decoration* and *Favourite Flowers.*

HYBRIDIZER: David Austin
SUITABILITY: all levels
AVAILABILITY: wide
STATURE & HABIT: 10 feet ×
   10 feet (warm climate);
   6 feet × 6 feet (cool climate)
FRAGRANCE: strong myrrh

USES: climber, tall shrub,
   cutting
PARENTAGE: 'Belle Isis' ×
   'Dainty Maid'
DISEASES: mildew, rust
DENOMINATION: None

Constance
Spry

COTTAGE ROSE

[*1991*]

This rose is proving to be a true garden treasure. Cooler weather brings out deeper colors that remind me of the swirl of a strawberry-raspberry parfait. Although this cultivar will need some time to settle into the garden, it does exhibit a truly Old Rose charm that one hopes for in English Roses. 'Cottage Rose' is one of the most Damask-like of this class.

Flowers form from round pink buds that open to 3½-inch blooms. The flowers are shallow-cupped, silky pink with a button eye that reveals just a hint of yellow in the center and are sweetly fragrant. New growth is light green and edged with red. The shrub produces thin, very thorny canes with light green foliage and lots of red prickles. The canes arch over from their own weight, adding to the Damask-like aspect of this rose. The repeat bloom is very good.

When given some shade, the color is much deeper. Try growing 'Cottage Rose' in groups of two or three shrubs. The canes will interlock and provide internal support. The dead petals do hang on, so it will be necessary to deadhead regularly.

'Cottage Rose' is named for its resemblance to roses found in old cotters' gardens.

HYBRIDIZER: David Austin
SUITABILITY: all levels
AVAILABILITY: wide
STATURE & HABIT: 5 feet ×
3 feet (warm climate); 3 feet
× 2½ feet (cool climate)
FRAGRANCE: sweet

USES: border, low hedge,
cutting
PARENTAGE: 'Wife of Bath' ×
'Mary Rose'
DISEASES: mildew, black spot
DENOMINATION: AUSglisten
PATENT: 8671

Cottage Rose

COUNTRY LIVING

[*1991*]

This cultivar has proved to be a disappointment. It seems to lack vitality and is very prone to downy mildew, which saps any strength it might have. Perennial optimists that we gardeners are, I have acquired a new plant to try again. My rule is to never judge a rose based on just one plant.

'Country Living' is a small shrub with smallish, medium green foliage. The full, 2½-inch, deeply cupped flowers are pink fading to white, often with a small green eye at the center, and lightly fragrant. Repeat bloom is an unknown factor as the bush has yet to show much zest. Another problem is that the flowers seem to ball and not open, even in hot weather. Cane dieback from cold winters has been reported, so some protection of grafted plants seems to be in order in areas susceptible to the problem. Own-root plants should be more winter-hardy.

Part of the problem is the fact that all plants that I have seen of this cultivar seem to be infected with downy mildew. Quite possibly, once the fungus is cleaned up, the plant will be worth growing. Downy mildew manifests itself as purple-black areas on stems and peduncles, starting off scattered and progressing until the entire cane is infected. Infected canes lose all vitality and usually die soon after complete infection. Not a pretty picture!

'Country Living' is named for the popular British magazine of the same name.

HYBRIDIZER: David Austin
SUITABILITY: intermediate
AVAILABILITY: mail order
STATURE & HABIT: 3 feet × 3 feet (warm climate); 3 feet × 2 feet (cool climate)
FRAGRANCE: light

USES: border
PARENTAGE: 'Wife of Bath' × 'Graham Thomas'
DISEASES: mildew, black spot
DENOMINATION: AUScountry
PATENT: 8777

Country Living

CRESSIDA

[*1983*]

To quote a well-known gardener, 'Cressida' is "a full-bosomed trollop of a rose." I love the fragrance; it reminds me of my grandmother's face cream. Just what else I like about this rose is difficult to put into words. The informal character of the flowers added to the wonderful fragrance makes 'Cressida' one of my personal favorites. Don't let the mildew fool you; it never stops blooming as long as it is kept deadheaded.

Large clusters of fat yellow buds produce 4½-inch, deeply cupped, very full globular flowers in a delicious shade of orange-apricot and creamy yellow, fading to white around the petal edges. The plant grows tall and is covered by lots of large red prickles. New basal canes are produced regularly and grow quickly to 6 feet or more. The dark green foliage, with five to seven leaflets, is very rugose when not covered by mildew.

Its Rugosa parent, 'Conrad Ferdinand Meyer,' has imparted great vigor to this cultivar and, as a grandchild of the Climbing Tea Rose 'Gloire de Dijon,' explains the lovely, soft apricot color of 'Cressida.' A double dose of Old Rose never hurt any self-respecting English Rose!

This cultivar is named for the passionate daughter of Calchas, a Trojan priest in Shakespeare's *Troilus and Cressida*.

HYBRIDIZER: David Austin
SUITABILITY: all levels
AVAILABILITY: mail order
STATURE & HABIT: 6 feet ×
  4 feet (warm climate);
  8 feet × 8 feet (cool climate)
FRAGRANCE: strong myrrh and
  fruity

USES: tall shrub, border,
  cutting
PARENTAGE: 'Conrad Ferdinand
  Meyer' × 'Chaucer'
DISEASE: mildew
DENOMINATION: AUScress

Cressida

CYMBELINE

[*1982*]

This rose tends to grow much wider than tall. It's possible that it will climb, but my experience is that it does not produce flowers except at the ends of the long canes. It's also possible that if it were planted with more growing space, its habit would improve. The flowers are attractive and the plant has good stamina. Add to this healthy disease-resistance, and 'Cymbeline' could make a respectable shrub for the right garden—just give him lots of space.

Austin describes the color of this rose as having an unusual gray-pink cast. To my eye, it does seem pink with just a slight tinge of lilac or gray. Fat, round pink buds are produced in big terminal clusters at the ends of long, arching canes. Flowers open to shallow-cupped, flat, very full, soft pink blossoms 3 to 4 or more inches across. Dark green glossy foliage blankets the plant and creates a stage for the blooms. New foliage is reddish with light green prickles, and the polished canes are smooth with scattered prickles. Fragrance is strong and fruity.

Self-pegging will most definitely improve this cultivar. Or you might try training it over a low fence or wall to see if it will break along the canes and produce bunches of flowering laterals.

Cymbeline is the king of Britain in William Shakespeare's tragicomedy of the same name.

HYBRIDIZER: David Austin
SUITABILITY: all levels
AVAILABILITY: limited
STATURE & HABIT: 6 feet ×
  8 feet (warm climate);
  4 feet × 5 feet (cool climate)
FRAGRANCE: strong and fruity

USES: low climber, border
PARENTAGE: seedling × 'Lilian
  Austin'
DISEASE: mildew
DENOMINATION: AUSlean

Cymbeline

DAPPLE DAWN

[*1983*]

If you like single-petaled roses, this one is for you. I actually prefer 'Dapple Dawn' to its parent 'Red Coat.' There is a certain subtle grace to 'Dapple Dawn' not found with the "in-your-face" scarlet of 'Red Coat.' Flowers are displayed all over this tall, robust shrub that is seldom out of bloom. Even the hips are attractive when they color up in the fall. It is hard to find fault with this rose.

The shrub can, with light pruning, reach quite large dimensions, though again it will be wider than tall. Pointed red buds in large terminal clusters open to single-petaled, warm pink, 4-inch flowers that are lighter on their edges. Petal reverse is a silvery pink. The base of the petals has a creamy yellow cast, and the centers are set off by bright golden stamens. At times, 'Dapple Dawn' will blanket itself with bloom; other times, it is as though a flock of pink butterflies are scattered all over the plant. Repeat bloom is excellent. New growth is edged with red and is quite robust.

This is the best of the single-flowered English Roses. Grow it as a large, freestanding shrub, or place a pair at the entrance to a garden room—you will not be sorry. Deadheading is important to keep a tidy appearance, but you can stop pruning in late summer or early fall, and the hips will provide an attractive winter display.

The name is from "The Windhover," a sonnet by the English poet Gerard Manley Hopkins.

HYBRIDIZER: David Austin
SUITABILITY: all levels
AVAILABILITY: mail order
STATURE & HABIT: 6 feet ×
  8 feet (warm climate);
  5 feet × 4 feet (cool climate)
FRAGRANCE: light

USES: border, accent shrub,
  hedge
PARENTAGE: sport of 'Red Coat'
DISEASE: black spot
DENOMINATION: none

Dapple Dawn

DOVE

[*1984*]

'Dove' is another low-growing shrub that ends up wider than it is tall. One of my favorite Austins, this cultivar engenders a garden mystery as the flowers progress through the various stages of development. Shown pictures in different stages of bloom, most people don't realize that they are all from the same rose.

Pointed pink buds resembling those of Hybrid Teas open to 3½-inch white flowers with blush centers. Flowers end up flat, full rosettes and are very fragrant with a Tea Rose scent. The foliage is medium green and glossy and covers the arching canes well; for me, this cultivar is seldom, if ever, bothered by disease, although mildew and black spot can be a problem in some areas of the country.

Almost always in flower, this is the most Tea-like of the Austin Roses. Try clustering several in the garden for maximum effect. The repeat bloom is so dependable that the plant seems to be in flower constantly. 'Dove' drops its petals cleanly and needs deadheading only after all the flowers in the large clusters have finished. Freshly dropped petals under the bush give the immediate area the look of a snowdrift.

HYBRIDIZER: David Austin

SUITABILITY: all levels

AVAILABILITY: mail order

STATURE & HABIT: 3 feet × 4 feet (warm climate); 2½ feet × 3 feet (cool climate)

FRAGRANCE: mild Tea Rose

USES: border, cutting

PARENTAGE: 'Wife of Bath' × seedling

DISEASES: mildew, black spot

DENOMINATION: AUSdove

Dove

ELLEN

[*1984*]

'Ellen' doesn't seem as robust as some of the other English Roses. She lacks strength and is vulnerable to cane dieback—a shame, as 'Ellen' can be quite spectacular. If you like this color, you might want to give her a try, but be forewarned—she is temperamental and doesn't settle into most gardens without a lot of work on the gardener's part. With this rose, patience is truly a virtue.

Tough, dark green, Rugosa-like foliage and plenty of large prickles cover the canes. The 4-inch orange-apricot flowers are deeply cupped and very fragrant. Blooms are produced on rather short stems and do need deadheading to keep the stems from dying back. Repeat bloom is not as good as some of the other roses in this color and class.

When first planted, this shrub grew to over 4 feet and literally covered itself with bloom. But over the years, it has slowly decreased in vitality and has shrunk to around 2 feet or so. It has, however, recently started to produce some new, stronger basal canes and may be on a comeback. The cheerful fruity fragrance is quite a plus, and for those who are up to a challenge, that might just be the deciding factor for growing this rose.

This cultivar is named for Ellen Drew, an Austin Nursery employee who retired in 1984.

HYBRIDIZER: David Austin
SUITABILITY: all levels
AVAILABILITY: wide
STATURE & HABIT: 4 feet ×
   3 feet (warm climate);
   4 feet × 4 feet (cool climate)
FRAGRANCE: strong rose

USES: border, container
PARENTAGE: 'Charles Austin' ×
   seedling
DISEASES: mildew, black spot
DENOMINATION: AUScup

Ellen

EMANUEL

[*1985*]

Over the years, this shrub has steadily improved to the point that it can be recommended to just about any rose lover at any level. When in full bloom, the self-pegged canes literally cover themselves with short-stemmed blossoms.

Foliage is medium sized, glossy dark green, and although it has a natural resistance to disease, you may want to take precautions in some areas of the country. Fat, round pink-and-yellow buds open to shallow-cupped flowers that are a soft pink with apricot centers. Blooms 3 inches across and full of petals are produced in clusters of three to five buds. 'Emanuel' has a wonderful fruity perfume that's a delightful change from the run-of-the-mill Hybrid Teas.

Although a tall bush, it never attains the proportions of some of its larger siblings and is an ideal candidate for self-pegging, which increases the number and frequency of flowers. Pegging or arching this shrub will encourage every bud eye to break and produce phenomenal clusters of flowers all along the arched canes. Instead of one cluster of three flowers at the top of 6 foot canes, you get twenty to thirty stems with clusters of flowers!

This cultivar is named for David and Elizabeth Emanuel, the English dress designers who designed Princess Diana's wedding dress in 1981.

HYBRIDIZER: David Austin
SUITABILITY: all levels
AVAILABILITY: mail order
STATURE & HABIT: 6 feet ×
   4 feet (warm climate);
   4 feet × 3 feet (cool climate)
FRAGRANCE: strong and fruity

USES: border, self-pegging,
   cutting
PARENTAGE: ('Chaucer' ×
   'Parade') × (seedling ×
   'Iceberg')
DISEASES: mildew, black spot
DENOMINATION: AUSuel

Emanuel

EMILY

[*1992*]

Why introduce another pink flower that looks so much like its parent 'Mary Rose'? The answer might be that 'Emily' is the "next generation." Slightly more compact, she seems to flower more profusely and longer, and her fragrance is truly out of this world.

Dark green foliage contrasts well with the 3½-inch flowers, which are produced in small clusters. Bloom formation is a shallow cup, opening blush pink with a button eye, and fading to white on the outer reflexed petals. There is an indescribable quality to the cupped bloom; the guard petals curve back, giving the blossom a charming petticoat effect. The shrub is exuberant and the flowers repeat well with a lovely, sweet, fruity fragrance.

A tall but not overpowering shrub, 'Emily' is best suited for the back of the border or clustered in groups of three or more for the impact of her massed bloom. I have seen some mildew early in the season and it can be a problem, but the plant does go on blooming and blooming. If you're looking for another pink rose, this is definitely one to try.

This rose is named for a character in "The Knight's Tale" whom Chaucer describes as being fairer than the lily or the May rose.

HYBRIDIZER: David Austin
SUITABILITY: all levels
AVAILABILITY: limited
STATURE & HABIT: 4 feet ×
3 feet (warm climate);
2½ feet × 2 feet (cool
climate)
FRAGRANCE: sweet and fruity

USES: border, cutting,
container
PARENTAGE: 'The Prioress' ×
'Mary Rose'
DISEASES: mildew, black spot
DENOMINATION: AUSburton
PATENT: 8838

Emily

ENGLISH ELEGANCE

[*1986*]

Although one of the few English Roses to actually climb, this rose is a bit of a disappointment—its foliage is just too sparse and too prone to disease. Some growers criticize its disorganized flower form, but that doesn't bother me as much as its lack of health.

Buds are red and yellow and round. Informally shaped 2- to 3-inch pink-to-salmon flowers with hints of yellow and copper are produced in small clusters on short stems. Flowers lack internal organization, with the center petals going in all directions. The scanty foliage is light green with red prickles. The flowers hold on long after they have finished, giving the plant quite an untidy look. Regular deadheading is a necessity, both to keep a clean look and to prevent dieback of the flowering stems. When regularly deadheaded, the repeat bloom is good. Mildew and black spot can be a problem, so be prepared for them.

This is one of those roses that require high culture: a deep organic mulch, regular feedings, and regular, deep irrigation are absolutely demanded. There is a certain charm to the blooms, but the informal, somewhat disorganized flowers are unlike any others in the group. Over time and with the right placement, 'English Elegance' will develop into a small climber. Allow it to fall over a wall, or self-peg it in the border.

HYBRIDIZER: David Austin
SUITABILITY: all levels
AVAILABILITY: mail order
STATURE & HABIT: 7 feet ×
   7 feet (warm climate);
   5 feet × 5 feet (cool climate)
FRAGRANCE: strong

USES: climber, large shrub
PARENTAGE: unlisted
DISEASES: mildew, black spot
DENOMINATION: AUSleaf
PATENT: 7557

English
Elegance

ENGLISH GARDEN

[*1986*]

By far, one of the most dependable of the low-growing English Roses. Most people overlook this outstanding cultivar when picking yellow flowers and select the much larger-growing 'Graham Thomas,' which is far less suitable for the small garden. Steady reliability is sometimes preferable over glitz and glitter.

Orange-yellow buds open to flat, shallow-cupped, 4-inch, pale yellow flowers that are a deeper yellow to apricot at the center. The color reminds me of the Old Noisette 'William Allen Richardson.' The fragrance is strong and fruity, and repeat bloom is truly outstanding. Foliage is light green and large, covering the low-growing shrub well. New canes are light green and smooth with a few red prickles. I have seen some rust and black spot on my plants.

The color and form of the flowers change with the season. One may see more pink than yellow in the early spring, and yellow will tend to predominate in the summer. Visitors have often challenged me as to the correct identity of the plants in my garden because of this changeability. So don't be too surprised if the flowers don't seem quite what you remembered from the pictures. Try planting 'English Garden' in groups of three; the display of blooms will light up any garden.

A number of complaints have been made regarding how huge the yellow English Roses can become, but this criticism is really aimed at 'Graham Thomas.' There are lower-growing yellow roses in this group that perform and bloom without producing huge growth, and 'English Garden' is certainly one of them. Be forewarned: Yellow roses tend to be not quite as cold-hardy as some of the other colors. You may even want to try this one in a pot.

HYBRIDIZER: David Austin

SUITABILITY: all levels

AVAILABILITY: available

STATURE & HABIT: 3 feet × 3 feet (warm climate); 3 feet × 3 feet (cool climate)

FRAGRANCE: strong and fruity

USES: border, cutting, container, partial shade

PARENTAGE: ('Lilian Austin' × seedling) × ('Iceberg' × 'Wife of Bath')

DISEASES: black spot, rust

DENOMINATION: AUSbuff

PATENT: 7214

*English
Garden*

EVELYN

[*1991*]

In the space of three months, the bushes of this cultivar grew from a foot tall when they were planted in Southern California to 6 feet tall. Because of this, they were pruned rather hard the following January to keep them a little more under control. Unfortunately, during the next year, the plants did not show the same vigor. Part of the problem seemed to have been root competition from a large Asian magnolia located next to the bed. Deep mulching and regular irrigation seem to have helped the situation, and 'Evelyn' is now a garden favorite.

Pointed yellow-orange buds open to fat, deeply cupped, 4-inch, intensely fragrant rosettes of soft yellow-apricot that slowly fade to pink with buffy yellow centers. The light green shiny foliage is susceptible to black spot. Plants are tall and upright with thorny canes that begin to arch over at the 6-foot mark. When cut back hard, the canes seem to have greater problems with dieback. This cultivar does require regular deadheading to encourage rebloom. New canes are deeply polished mahogany with ruby red prickles.

Though from the same line as 'Jayne Austin' and 'Sweet Juliet,' 'Evelyn' has become more popular than those two partly because her much larger flowers are better proportioned to the shrub. Do take care where you site this rose, however; she does not seem to be able to tolerate shade well at all.

According to David Austin, 'Evelyn' was selected by the perfumers Crabtree & Evelyn because of her intense fragrance, to mark the introduction of a new range of rose toiletries from that company. The name is pronounced EVE-lynn.

HYBRIDIZER: David Austin
SUITABILITY: all levels
AVAILABILITY: wide
STATURE & HABIT: 6 feet ×
  6 feet (warm climate);
  3 feet × 3 feet (cool climate)
FRAGRANCE: strong and fruity

USES: border, cutting
PARENTAGE: 'Graham Thomas'
  × 'Tamora'
DISEASES: mildew, black spot
DENOMINATION: AUSsaucer
PATENT: 8680

Evelyn

FAIR BIANCA

[*1982*]

It seems that small-growing English Roses are few and far between compared to the larger, more dynamic cultivars released to date. 'Fair Bianca' is one that has a lot going for it: good foliage; short, upright growth; and pure white, cupped, fragrant flowers that cut well and last in bouquets.

Fat reddish yellow buds open to 3-inch, deeply cupped, pure white flowers produced in large terminal clusters. The petals swirl around a green eye in the manner of that great Old Damask 'Madame Hardy.' The strong myrrh fragrance has a hint of fruit to my nose. The low-growing plant is upright with good, dark green foliage. The canes are covered with prickles very much like those of Gallica Roses; in fact, this plant reminds me of that class of OGRs, only this one blooms and blooms. Be prepared for mildew and black spot as this cultivar can have some early on. In some areas, rust can be a problem as well. An ounce of prevention will be important but well worth the effort if you love white roses as much as I do.

'Fair Bianca' is a good rose for the smaller garden, or to try in a pot. One commercial grower uses this cultivar for the cut-flower trade—it is cut in the bud stage and shipped all over the country. Removed in this way, the blooms open slowly and last particularly long.

Bianca was the sweet sister of Katherina, the shrew, in *The Taming of the Shrew.*

HYBRIDIZER: David Austin
SUITABILITY: all levels
AVAILABILITY: wide
STATURE & HABIT: 3 feet ×
  3 feet (warm climate);
  3 feet × 4 feet (cool climate)
FRAGRANCE: myrrh

USES: border, container,
  cutting
PARENTAGE: unlisted
DISEASES: mildew, black spot,
  rust
DENOMINATION: AUSca

*Fair
Bianca*

FRANCINE AUSTIN

[*1988*]

One of the more unique cultivars in growth habit and bloom of all the English Roses, this shrub grows wider than tall, to 6 feet or more across, making it a potential ground cover. The growth and flower of 'Francine Austin' are very typical of the early, bushy Noisettes—as one would expect, considering her parentage.

Pure white flowers, 2 inches across and showing yellow stamens at the centers, are produced from small pink buds. Flowers are produced in large, very fragrant, panicled sprays. 'Francine Austin' just blooms and blooms. The white flowers are displayed to perfection against the large, dark green, long and pointed foliage; reddish prickles are numerous. In cool weather, the white flowers take on a pinkish cast.

Allow 'Francine Austin' to tumble over a low wall or climb along a fence; or buy this cultivar as a standard, or tree rose, and the long, arching canes will create a weeping effect. Used as a ground cover, the bending canes will intertwine, spilling lovely white petals all over the garden. To achieve this effect, be sure to plant the bushes about 3 feet apart; otherwise, 4- to 5-foot spacing will do.

Winter hardiness might be of concern, considering this rose's Noisette parentage—the Noisette Roses are not truly winter-hardy in the coldest parts of our country. North of the Sunbelt, plan to give her some extra protection during the coldest months.

This rose is named for an Austin daughter-in-law.

HYBRIDIZER: David Austin
SUITABILITY: all levels
AVAILABILITY: limited
STATURE & HABIT: 3 feet ×
   6 feet (warm climate);
   3 feet × 4 feet (cool climate)
FRAGRANCE: light

USES: border, ground cover,
   container
PARENTAGE: 'Alister Stella
   Gray' × 'Ballerina'
DISEASES: none of note
DENOMINATION: AUSram
PATENT: 8156

Francine Austin

GERTRUDE JEKYLL

[*1986*]

M**y first experience with 'Gertude Jekyll' was back in 1987, when I planted her in my entry border garden. Between March and August, she grew to over 10 feet tall! "Galloping Gerty," as we now prefer to call her, is a rose that everyone wants to grow and should grow—provided they can make provisions and allowances for her vitality and size. Another excellent reason to grow her is the perfume. Austin claims this is the most fragrant of all the English Roses.

Large, fat pink buds open to 4½-inch flowers of truly wonderful Old Rose formation. Blooms are flat and full of quartered petals in an exquisite shade of warm pink. Flowers are produced in terminal clusters of three to six buds. When the plant is allowed to attain its full size, the repeat bloom is best described as sporadic, but it can, of course, be much improved by self-pegging. Tall, very thorny canes are covered with long, pointed, dark green foliage, which makes a foil for the blossoms.

The daunting size of this cultivar can be reduced by hard pruning. I know of one gardener who kept hers down to around 18 inches! It is not recommended that anyone try this, but my friend did get incredibly long stems when she cut flowers for the house. Self-pegging was originally created to control 'Gertrude Jekyll' and is the recommended size/space remedy for this cultivar. The plant can be contained in a 4- by 4-foot space using this approach.

In every respect, 'Gertrude Jekyll' is very similar to her Portland Rose parent, 'Comte de Chambord'—she's merely taller and more hardy. The double dose of Old Rose parentage is apparent in the classic charms of her blooms and fragrance.

One of the most influential garden designers of the early twentieth century, Gertrude Jekyll (pronounced JEE-kul) was the author of a number of gardening books, including *Roses for English Gardens.*

HYBRIDIZER: David Austin
SUITABILITY: all levels
AVAILABILITY: wide
STATURE & HABIT: 10 feet × 6 feet (warm climate); 4 feet × 3½ feet (cool climate)
FRAGRANCE: strong Old Rose

USES: back of border, self-pegging, cutting
PARENTAGE: 'Wife of Bath' × 'Comte de Chambord'
DISEASES: mildew, black spot
DENOMINATION: AUSbord
PATENT: 6220

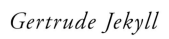

Gertrude Jekyll

GLAMIS CASTLE

[*1992*]

A first-rate introduction, this low-growing bush is not one of those roses you can just stick in the ground, stand back, and watch grow to unprecedented heights. It requires high culture; specifically, generous mulching and regular feedings and irrigations are absolutely essential, at least until the shrub is well-established. But once ensconced, 'Glamis Castle' will repay all your efforts with bouquets of lovely white blossoms.

Round buds produce 2½- to 3-inch, pure white flowers with creamy centers, opening to globular, cupped, and ruffled blooms that have a strong, sweet fragrance. Repeat bloom seems to be good. New growth, edged with red, is very prickly. Mature foliage is deep green, small, and rounded, and can have mild problems with both mildew and black spot. While this cultivar is establishing itself, the flowers will be small, but the size improves with age.

This new cultivar will have a rather limited introduction in this country until gardeners demand that growers offer it on their lists. Although it's not as exuberant or as large-flowered as some of the other white English Roses, 'Glamis Castle' deserves a place in the garden. It would be great in a container or clustered in groups of three as an accent.

Glamis Castle is the home of the Queen Mother and the setting of Shakespeare's *Macbeth.* True to English style, the correct pronunciation of this cultivar is, as the castle, not GLAM-us but GLAMS.

HYBRIDIZER: David Austin
SUITABILITY: all levels
AVAILABILITY: limited
STATURE & HABIT: 3 feet ×
   3 feet (warm climate); 3 feet
   × 2½ feet (cool climate)
FRAGRANCE: sweet

USES: border, bedding,
   container, partial shade
PARENTAGE: 'Graham Thomas'
   × 'Mary Rose'
DISEASES: mildew, black spot
DENOMINATION: AUSlevel
PATENT: 8765

Glamis Castle

GOLDEN CELEBRATION

[*1992*]

Although introduced in the U.K. in 1992, this cultivar has not been widely available on this side of the Atlantic until now. A five-year time lag may seem a bit long, but there is a two-year U.S. quarantine that all European cultivars must pass. Then there's the time it takes to increase plant stocks to the point where a cultivar can be put on the retail market. The Austin people are well aware of the problem and are making adjustments they hope will bring their new introductions to market in the U.S. much sooner after their U.K. premiere.

The fat, round, red-and-yellow buds of 'Golden Celebration' open to 3½-inch, deeply cupped, fully petaled flowers that hold their rich golden yellow color very well. The scent is strong and spicy, mixed with both fruit and Tea Rose aromas. Blooms sometimes display a button eye, and the petals are notched. New growth is shiny light green, and the new canes are a smooth mahogany and almost thornless. Foliage can burn in the summer sun, so some protection from the hottest sun is in order. The repeat bloom is good, and 'Golden Celebration' doesn't seem to have any major problem with disease, although yellow roses can be more susceptible to black spot. Where this disease is a problem, it would be wise to take appropriate precautions.

The color is darker and more golden than that of 'Graham Thomas.' Although one hopes it does not reach the monumental proportions of that great cultivar, the odds are that 'Golden Celebration' will grow taller than its catalog description. This rose is unusually brilliant and will do wonders brightening up a drab corner of your garden.

HYBRIDIZER: David Austin
SUITABILITY: all levels
AVAILABILITY: limited
STATURE & HABIT: 4 feet ×
    4 feet (warm climate);
    4 feet × 4 feet (cool climate)
FRAGRANCE: strong

USES: border, container,
    cutting
PARENTAGE: 'Charles Austin' ×
    'Abraham Darby'
DISEASES: mildew, black spot
DENOMINATION: AUSgold
PATENT: 8688

Golden Celebration

GRAHAM THOMAS

[*1983*]

Without a doubt, this cultivar is one of the five or six most popular and recognizable of the English Roses introduced to date. The unique color clearly places it among a rare few. But 'Graham Thomas' is not for the faint of heart—the shrub can achieve 10 feet or more in height. A real quandary of a rose, one must ponder how to keep it under control *and* get it to rebloom. Self-pegging has solved this problem in my garden. Those who have grown this cultivar in climate zones other than my own swear that it stays under 5 feet and blooms constantly.

Round red-and-yellow buds open to shallow-cupped, buttery yellow, 3½-inch flowers, wonderfully scented with a fruity Tea Rose perfume. The coloring, when compared to contemporary Hybrid Teas, is so subtle as to seem almost subliminal. The golden yellow petals often hint at a blush of red-gold with darker gold shadings to the centers. There is only a glimpse of the stamens as the petals reflex. Flowers are produced in terminal clusters of seven to eight on long, arching canes that are well-covered with shiny, dark green, leathery foliage. New growth is light green edged red with large green prickles. Stop deadheading in fall for a large crop of elegant, round yellow hips.

With 'Iceberg' as one of his parents, you can expect good, disease-resistant foliage and a tolerance of shade. In fact, I have planted a bed in dappled shade and the shrub seems to be responding quite well. Elsewhere in warm-climate zones, self-pegging is the best answer for this adamant grower.

This amazing cultivar is named for Graham Stuart Thomas, the British Old Rose expert and author of *The Graham Stuart Thomas Rose Book,* which comprises his trilogy, *The Old Shrub Roses, Shrub Roses of Today,* and *Climbing Roses Old and New.*

HYBRIDIZER: David Austin
SUITABILITY: all levels
AVAILABILITY: wide
STATURE & HABIT: 10 feet ×
   8 feet (warm climate);
   5 feet × 4 feet (cool climate)
FRAGRANCE: strong Tea Rose

USES: back of border,
   self-pegging, cutting, partial
   shade
PARENTAGE: 'Charles Austin' ×
   ('Iceberg' × seedling)
DISEASE: mildew
DENOMINATION: AUSmas

*Graham
Thomas*

HAPPY CHILD

[*1993*]

Nothing about the parents of this cultivar indicates that a yellow of such delicate coloration, or any yellow for that matter, should be produced. The color is intense.

This plant has been rather slow to develop and somewhat prone to cane dieback. Disbud or remove flowers of new roses when they are first planted, a difficult operation when one really wants to see the flowers. However, especially for own-root plants, disbudding through two or three flowering cycles will allow the plant to build up strength and produce a much better bush in the end—if you can stand the suspense.

Everything about this cultivar is decidedly more modern than the average English Rose. Bright yellow buds open to 3½-inch, brilliant yellow flowers. The petals reflex back, revealing perfect rosette centers. The flowers do fade rather quickly to pale yellow, and finally to buff white. The foliage is shiny, light green, and lush, making a good contrast to the elegant, bright yellow flowers. Growth is slow but the bush should grow to 2 to 3 feet in a few seasons. Keeping this child happy requires extra care and cultivation. Try placing this rose so that it receives some protection from the hottest sun.

Austin named the cultivar in aid of Population Concern, which raises funds for Planned Parenthood around the world.

HYBRIDIZER: David Austin
SUITABILITY: all levels
AVAILABILITY: limited
STATURE & HABIT: 2 feet ×
  2 feet (warm climate);
  3½ feet × 3 feet (cool climate)
FRAGRANCE: sweet and fruity

USES: border, cutting, partial
  shade
PARENTAGE: (seedling ×
  'Iceberg') × 'Hero'
DISEASES: mildew, black spot
DENOMINATION: AUScomp
PATENT: 9007

Happy Child

HERITAGE

[*1984*]

O ften touted as one of the finest English Roses, this cultivar has remained among the top five or six best-selling of the group for some time. David Austin himself thinks that it is one of his most beautiful. Over the years, 'Heritage' has proved to be somewhat difficult to grow to perfection. Quite often the foliage, which at most times is perfect, burns in the hot summer sun, and the bush truly resents hard pruning. The foliage is also on the sparse side—I prefer plants that are well-covered with lush green foliage as a background for the flowers. Friends who have grown 'Heritage' in cooler areas, though, have been quite happy with it. The cupped flowers remind me of the Old Alba Rose 'Maiden's Blush' and are just as heart-melting as the best of the classic Old Roses.

Round red buds produce clusters of 3-inch, deeply cupped, blush pink flowers. The scent is sweet and fruity. New growth is bronze and the almost thornless canes are light green turning to dark green as they age. For me, the foliage is clean and resistant to most diseases, but in other parts of the country, be prepared for some problems with disease.

'Heritage' is a seductive rose and another of the English Roses with 'Iceberg' in its background. It is named for its purity of bloom and Old Rose form.

HYBRIDIZER: David Austin
SUITABILITY: all levels
AVAILABILITY: wide
STATURE & HABIT: 6 feet ×
4 feet (warm climate);
4 feet × 4 feet (cool climate)
FRAGRANCE: strong

USES: border, hedge, low
climber, cutting, partial
shade
PARENTAGE: seedling ×
('Iceberg' × 'Wife of Bath')
DISEASES: mildew, rust
DENOMINATION: AUSblush

Heritage

HERO

[*1982*]

There are sixty plants of this rose in my garden, designed as a mass planting edging an important central walkway, so I guess you could say that 'Hero' might be one of my favorite English Roses. The bush is a bit rangy-growing with a rather open habit, but it literally covers itself with huge, exquisitely heartbreaking, fragrant blossoms.

Large terminal clusters of pointed red buds open to 4-inch globular flowers. Glowing pink petals reflex back to reveal golden yellow centers with masses of yellow stamens and contrasting red pistils. The notched petals are so large that the semi-double flowers appear to be double at first. They loosen to shallow cups as they age, and the color fades to a soft pink. The fragrance is a strong myrrh scent. The light green new growth is edged with bronze and covered with green and red prickles. There is a gray tone to the green of the foliage, which is produced in five to seven leaflets. The long canes will bend out to 5 or 6 feet, but the shrub can be kept to 3 or 4 feet. Do follow Austin's advice and plant a group of two or three about 1½ to 2 feet apart, allowing them to intertwine.

One could not ask more from a rose. 'Hero' is almost never out of bloom, and the fragrance is exquisite. It does have a mild problem with rust, so take precautions to combat that nastiness.

Hero, a priestess of Aphrodite, was the beloved of Leander.

HYBRIDIZER: David Austin
SUITABILITY: all levels
AVAILABILITY: mail order
STATURE & HABIT: 4 feet ×
   5 feet (warm climate);
   5 feet × 4 feet (cool climate)
FRAGRANCE: strong myrrh

USES: border, hedge, cutting
PARENTAGE: 'The Prioress' ×
   seedling
DISEASES: mildew, rust
DENOMINATION: AUShero

Hero

HILDA MURRELL

[*1984*]

With all the fine pink English Roses introduced to date, it's easy to overlook one. This cultivar, although not of the first order, can be worth growing if only for its occasionally produced, sweetly fragrant flowers. Austin includes 'Hilda Murrell' (pronounced Myrrh-ELL) among his summer-flowering roses; she does, however, seem to have a dependable fall rebloom in the more temperate zones of the United States.

Dark red buds produce warm pink flowers with ruffled edges; the 4-inch flowers have a shallow-cupped shape, with the outer petals reflexing back quite widely, though the blooms are very full and flat. The fragrance is strong and sweetly scented of Damask Rose. New growth is reddish green with dark red prickles. A tall, upright, thorny bush, 'Hilda Murrell' does have ample rugose, seven-leaflet foliage. The canes are embellished with a multitude of cardinal red prickles. In most climates, you will need to be ready to protect this rose from mildew and rust.

Although a tall grower, 'Hilda Murrell' can withstand hard pruning to keep her in bounds. The plant takes on a rather upright and tough appearance that's best if used in the back of the border; the flowers do add a certain charm when the shrub is allowed to grow full size.

The name commemorates a pioneer in the reintroduction of Old Roses who lived near David Austin's nursery.

HYBRIDIZER: David Austin
SUITABILITY: all levels
AVAILABILITY: limited
STATURE & HABIT: 6 feet ×
  3 feet (warm climate);
  4 feet × 4 feet (cool climate)
FRAGRANCE: strong Damask

USES: border, tall hedge, cutting
PARENTAGE: seedling ×
  ('Parade' × 'Chaucer')
DISEASES: mildew, rust
DENOMINATION: AUSmurr

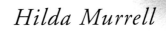

Hilda Murrell

HUNTINGTON'S HERO

[*1995*]

This unique flower was discovered growing on one of sixty plants of 'Hero' in The Huntington Botanical Garden's rose collection in San Marino, California. It was in a form known as a bud sport, or mutation. Three cuttings were struck from the cane that sported; two reverted back to the parent, 'Hero,' and only the third cutting remained true to the mutation.

'Huntington's Hero' differs from its parent in that the 3-inch, semi-double blooms have only two or three rows of notched petals that open out of their shallow-cupped form to a much more open flower, displaying bright golden stamens and red pistils right from the beginning. The flower color is pale pink to (more rarely) coral pink; sometimes, it's so pale as to be almost white with an overall jaundice blush. In the heat of summer, the blooms open a pale buff yellow. The elegantly pointed buds are yellowish coral with a distinctive red stripe. There is a definite bluish cast to the gray-green foliage, with bright red prickles well spaced along the canes. Strongly scented with myrrh and nutmeg, the flowers are produced in terminal clusters on short, curving canes.

So far this cultivar seems to resist most diseases, and the foliage clothes the plant well, displaying crop after crop of blooms above plentiful blue-green leaves. Growth seems to be very much like its parent, rather open and wide at first, to about 3 to 4 feet high and 5 feet wide. Plant two or three bushes about 1½ feet apart, and they will grow into each other, making a lovely display.

'Huntington's Hero' commemorates the seventy-fifth anniversary of Henry Edwards Huntington's founding of The Huntington Library in 1919. The Huntington Rose Garden displays nearly two thousand different species and cultivars from all periods of rose development, and includes one of the largest collections of David Austin's English Roses in North America.

HYBRIDIZER: Clair Martin
SUITABILITY: all levels
AVAILABILITY: limited
STATURE & HABIT: 4 feet ×
  5 feet (warm climate);
  3 feet × 4 feet (cool climate)
FRAGRANCE: strong myrrh

USES: border, hedge
PARENTAGE: sport of 'Hero'
DISEASES: none of note
DENOMINATION: MARmy

*Huntington's
Hero*

JAQUENETTA

[*1983*]

This is a rather hard-to-find single-flowering English Rose, but it can be worth the trouble of searching out a source. The five-petaled flowers have a seductive allure that quite overpowers the most jaded of gardeners. Be aware that 'Jaquenetta' is probably not very winter-hardy, so take the appropriate precautions in colder zones.

Flowers are produced in profuse clusters and can be as much as 4 inches across. In some climates, single roses often produce more than one row of petals, giving the impression that they are semi-double; but in more seasonal parts of the United States, 'Jaquenetta' will retain its five-petaled singularity. Pointed buds are copper-colored; the flowers open from peachy apricot to copper-orange, with a strong, delicious fruity scent. New growth is light green with small red prickles. Dark green foliage makes a good contrast to the flowers, although mildew and rust can be a problem. Flowers are produced in large clusters at the cane tips, and the shrub is rather open in growth, making it wider than tall.

The plant repeats very well, but the flowers are somewhat quick to fade. The main fault of this cultivar, like most of Austin's single roses, is that the flowers open only one flower at a time per cluster.

As to the name, Jaquenetta was a country wench in Shakespeare's *Love's Labours Lost.*

HYBRIDIZER: David Austin
SUITABILITY: connoisseur
AVAILABILITY: limited
STATURE & HABIT: 4 feet ×
  5 feet (warm climate);
  4 feet × 4 feet (cool climate)
FRAGRANCE: strong fruity

USES: border, cutting
PARENTAGE: seedling ×
  'Charles Austin'
DISEASES: mildew, rust
DENOMINATION: none

Jaquenetta

JAYNE AUSTIN

[*1990*]

A large shrub with small flowers, this cultivar reminds me a good deal of its parent 'Graham Thomas.' The foliage is often marred by mildew in cool, moist weather, and in the heat of summer it tends to burn; but given enough water and care, 'Jayne Austin' can produce some rather charming blossoms.

Apricot-yellow buds open to 2-inch, fully petaled, cupped flowers of soft yellow deepening toward the center and displaying a charming button eye. The blooms have a delightful spicy fragrance. When not spoiled by mildew, the foliage is dark green and bountiful. The tall, bowing canes are well-armed with mean, blood red prickles.

'Jayne Austin' is also quite similar to 'Sweet Juliet,' and like that cultivar, she is rather stingy with her flowers. David Austin feels that this plant has inherited its Noisette-like characteristics from one of its grandparents, 'Gloire de Dijon.' As with many of the yellow English Roses, it would be best to provide her with some extra protection against the coldest winters.

This rose is named for an Austin daughter-in-law.

HYBRIDIZER: David Austin
SUITABILITY: all levels
AVAILABILITY: mail order
STATURE & HABIT: 6 feet ×
  3 feet (warm climate);
  3 feet × 2 feet (cool climate)
FRAGRANCE: strong, spicy

USES: self-pegging, back of
  border, cutting
PARENTAGE: 'Graham Thomas'
  × 'Tamora'
DISEASES: mildew, rust
DENOMINATION: AUSbreak
PATENT: 8682

Jayne Austin

KATHRYN MORLEY

[*1990*]

O n the tallish side, 'Kathryn Morley' would best be placed toward the back of a border or against a wall. A real charmer in the garden, she reminds me of a tall 'Chaucer,' with all that cultivar's grace of flower but less of its penchant for mildew.

Bulbous scarlet buds produce blossoms that open to 3½-inch, shallow-cupped, cameo pink flowers with coral pink centers opening just enough to flaunt the saffrony stamens. The petals are ruffled and notched, curling back at the tips; outer guard petals reflex back and are much lighter, eventually fading to the palest white-pink. The repeat bloom is good for a flower of this size and the fragrance sweet and strong. The foliage is dark green and canes are sheathed with large red prickles. There has been some mildew on this cultivar, but not enough to present a problem.

Self-pegging will help contain this robust plant within a manageable space and encourage her to produce even more abundant clusters of flowers.

This rose was named by a couple who bought that right at a charity auction. Their daughter Kathryn had died at the age of eighteen.

HYBRIDIZER: David Austin
SUITABILITY: all levels
AVAILABILITY: wide
STATURE & HABIT: 6 to 8 feet
    × 3 feet (warm climate);
    3½ feet × 3½ feet (cool
    climate)
FRAGRANCE: strong and sweet

USES: tall shrub, climber,
    cutting
PARENTAGE: 'Mary Rose' ×
    'Chaucer'
DISEASE: mildew
DENOMINATION: AUSclub
PATENT: 8814

Kathryn Morley

L. D. BRAITHWAITE

[*1988*]

Almost every garden can stand a shot of red, but a dependable, healthy, bright red had been lacking among the English Roses until the introduction of 'L. D. Braithwaite.' This is a robust, somewhat open-growing shrub that can be a bit sparse on foliage. Hard pruning and deadheading may help keep it within bounds and encourage more foliage growth.

Burgundy bud orbs open to 4-inch flowers, the outer petals of which reflex back in the manner of the great 'Mary Rose,' and the flowers finish up in a pristine rosette shape. They are the brightest crimson red color and carry a light rose fragrance. The color ages without turning to the blue side of red, although in the heat of summer the crimson red flowers will age to a reddish pink. New growth has a bronze cast, and the light green canes are blanketed with green prickles of all shapes and sizes. Leaves are produced in sets of five to seven leaflets. The shrub can get tall, but it can usually be kept to 4 or 5 feet in height as well as width. Disease doesn't seem to be a problem, and the repeat bloom is very dependable.

Don't let this mouthful of a moniker turn you off this excellent rose. Leonard Dudley Braithwaite is David Austin's father-in-law, and you just don't honor in-laws with poor roses.

HYBRIDIZER: David Austin
SUITABILITY: all levels
AVAILABILITY: wide
STATURE & HABIT: 5 feet ×
5 feet (warm climate);
3½ feet × 3½ feet (cool
climate)
FRAGRANCE: light

USES: border, cutting
PARENTAGE: 'Mary Rose' ×
'The Squire'
DISEASES: mildew, black spot
DENOMINATION: AUScrim
PATENT: 8154

L.D. Braithwaite

LEANDER

[*1982*]

L ike 'Cymbeline,' 'Leander' shares a problem with others of the same habit: It grows much wider than tall, and unless self-pegged, it flowers only at the ends of the long, sinuous canes. Self-pegging will help to control the size and encourage more flower production. Otherwise, this is definitely a rose for a low wall or fence where the arching canes can be trained to display the charming flowers to their utmost.

Bulging, round orange-red buds are produced in clusters of three. The just-opening buds, clustered as they are at the ends of bowing branches, remind me of bunches of grapes. These become 2½-inch orange-apricot, shallow-cupped, strongly scented flowers that are displayed beautifully against dark green, shiny foliage. New growth and canes are bronze with many dark vermilion prickles. Although the dark green foliage has good disease-resistance, it can be prone to a bit of mildew. The repeat bloom is good, however. At times, 'Leander' looks very much like a smaller-flowered version of 'Charles Austin.' The blooms age to a soft peachy pink, which can make a startling contrast to the orange-apricot of the newly opened flowers.

Leander was the Greek youth of legend who swam the Hellespont nightly to visit his beloved, Hero; during one arduous crossing, he became exhausted and drowned.

HYBRIDIZER: David Austin
SUITABILITY: all levels
AVAILABILITY: mail order
STATURE & HABIT: 6 feet ×
  8 feet (warm climate);
  6 feet × 5 feet (cool climate)
FRAGRANCE: strong

USES: climber
PARENTAGE: 'Charles Austin' ×
  seedling
DISEASE: mildew
DENOMINATION: AUSlea

Leander

LILAC ROSE

[*1990*]

The problem with including a color in the name of a cultivar is that it should live up to the name. In the warmer parts of the United States, the only lilac to be seen in this flower is during the coolest spring weather. The rest of the year, it's just another pink. The flowers are large and fragrant, and they do repeat well, but you'll be disappointed if you live in a temperate zone and you're searching specifically for a lilac-colored rose. It is quite possible that the lilac color will show up better if the plant is given some protection from the midday sun.

Bulging, round pink buds open to 3-inch, shallow-cupped, soft pink flowers that hold their cupped shape and open just enough to display some stamens at the center. The blooms look as though they have been crafted from crepe paper. New growth is light green edged with red and darkens to gray-green with small red prickles. The dark green foliage does have some problem with mildew, rust, and black spot.

So far this cultivar has proved to be rather low growing, maybe reaching to 3 feet, but it has taken three years to do so. 'Charles Rennie Mackintosh' is a much better plant, and more dependable in hot weather as far as the lilac color. In areas where the sun is not quite as intense and the summers are a bit cooler, the color of 'Lilac Rose' should be everything one wishes of a lilac-colored rose.

HYBRIDIZER: David Austin
SUITABILITY: all levels
AVAILABILITY: mail order
STATURE & HABIT: 3 feet ×
   3 feet (warm climate);
   3 feet × 2 feet (cool climate)
FRAGRANCE: strong

USES: border, cutting,
   container
PARENTAGE: seedling × 'Hero'
DISEASES: mildew, black spot,
   rust
DENOMINATION AUSlilac
PATENT: 8837

Lilac Rose

LILIAN AUSTIN

[*1973*]

There is a very modern look to the flowers of this English Rose. The growth pattern and appearance is much like that of a Floribunda. The shrub has lax canes, and self-pegging will help restrain the bush.

Fat tomato-red buds open to huge 4-inch, cupped, pompon-shaped flowers. The color is glowing pink to salmon with yellow and orange tones, and the petals open up to reveal bright gold stamens at the center. The large, informally shaped flowers are quite reminiscent of peonies; the fragrance mild and fruity. New growth is edged with red. Foliage is dark green, and leaves are typically produced with five to seven leaflets. Pale red-green prickles sheath the procumbent canes. This cultivar has remarkably clean and disease-free foliage on a shrub that repeats well; it is simply spectacular in a mass planting.

The color of 'Lilian Austin' has been a matter of discussion for some time. There are times when the flowers have a strong glow of salmon to them; then at other times, the blooms take on pink tones with hints of apricot and yellow. There are just three bushes of 'Lilian Austin' planted across the front of a 15-foot bed in my 3-acre garden. As an experiment, the spanning, very thorny canes have been woven into each other to make a continous hedge. The stunning display of bloom that has resulted can be seen from across the entire garden. So my recommendation would be that you plant this cultivar in groupings of three or more to get the best effect.

Lilian Austin is David Austin's mother.

HYBRIDIZER: David Austin
SUITABILITY: all levels
AVAILABILITY: mail order
STATURE & HABIT: 3 feet ×
  5 feet (warm climate);
  4 feet × 4 feet (cool climate)
FRAGRANCE: mild and fruity

USES: border, hedge
PARENTAGE: 'Aloha' ×
  'The Yeoman'
DISEASE: mild black spot
DENOMINATION: AUSli

Lilian Austin

LORDLY OBERON

[*1982*]

A truly stately rose, 'Lordly Oberon' produces long, elegant canes tipped with clusters of sweetly perfumed blossoms. Vigorous growth is fine if one is prepared for it, but in my first experience with this cultivar, the bushes were planted much too close, causing them to grow so tall that they shaded out their neighbors. Self-pegging will help control Oberon's overpowering exuberance and allow this rose to be grown within a much more modest space.

Oval cream and pink buds open to old-fashioned blush to white cupped flowers produced at the ends of 10-foot-long canes. Foliage is large and dark green and the canes are well-equipped with wicked, dark red prickles. The foliage can be a bit too prone to mildew in regions with that problem, and in cool, wet weather, the flowers can be spoiled and misshapen by balling, so do take this into consideration. 'Lordly Oberon' will flower much better in the more arid, desertlike climates of the West and Southwest. Flowers are produced in large clusters at the tips of the tall canes, so self-pegging will not only help control the ultimate height of this rose but will also encourage all the bud eyes along the cane to break and produce flowering shoots. Instead of producing one cluster at the tip of the cane, self-pegging 'Lordly Oberon' will then produce up to fifteen or thirty clusters of flowers along the cane.

Large cupped flowers virtually blanket the plant at peak bloom, and the flowers cut and hold beautifully in bouquets. The secret for cutting large, fully petaled roses like 'Lordly Oberon' is to wait until the flowers are about half open before cutting, and then to condition the flowers overnight by placing them in deep, warm water almost all the way up to the blooms.

Oberon is the king of the fairies in *A Midsummer Night's Dream.*

HYBRIDIZER: David Austin
SUITABILITY: intermediate
AVAILABILITY: mail order
STATURE & HABIT: 10 feet ×
  6 feet (warm climate);
  4 feet × 4 feet (cool climate)
FRAGRANCE: sweet

USES: tall shrub
PARENTAGE: 'Chaucer' × seedling
DISEASES: mildew, rust
DENOMINATION: AUSron

Lordly Oberon

LUCETTA

[*1983*]

This rose can be grown either as a freestanding shrub or as a small Pillar Rose, and it works beautifully either way. Many gardens simply scream out for Climbing Roses, or Pillar Roses—essentially, low to medium roses that flower from the ground up. Consider spicing up your own garden with some structural and height variations. Training the long, drooping canes of 'Lucetta' to spiral up a tripod or pillar will add an interesting dimension to the landscape.

Peachy pink buds open to large, teacup-shaped flowers 5 to 6 inches across. The semi-double blooms are shell pink with a hint of saffron at the base of lovely scalloped and ruffled petals. New growth is edged in red and produced in leaves of seven leaflets cast dark green. Canes carry the requisite red-tipped green prickles along their length. As with many newly planted roses, repeat bloom can be sparse until the plant is well established. The long, supple canes can be trained easily by self-pegging.

In many ways, this charming rose is just looking for the right spot in the garden. If you have the room, try planting two or three in a close cluster to take advantage of the lax growth habit. The plants will intertwine and make a large, self-supporting mound of flowers.

Lucetta was a lady-in-waiting to Julia in Shakespeare's *The Two Gentlemen of Verona.*

HYBRIDIZER: David Austin

SUITABILITY: all levels

AVAILABILITY: mail order

STATURE & HABIT: 6 to 8 feet
× 6 feet (warm climate);
4 feet × 4 feet (cool climate)

FRAGRANCE: strong

USES: tall shrub, climber,
cutting, partial shade

PARENTAGE: unknown

DISEASES: none of note

DENOMINATION: AUSemi

Lucetta

MARY ROSE

[*1983*]

'Mary Rose,' one of the top five or six English Roses, is truly magnificent. The flowers are every bit the quintessential old-fashioned Damask Rose on a modern repeat-flowering bush. One could easily imagine it planted in a formal garden of yesteryear.

Stout ruby buds are produced in clusters from the ground up. The 3-inch full-cupped, lightly fragrant, iridescent pink flowers retain their cupped form throughout their life, while the outer petals reflex back, giving the blooms the look of having an old-fashioned petticoat. New growth is light green maturing to dark green, with the usually five leaflets having good resistance to mildew. Canes are heavily sprinkled with pale to red prickles.

This rose was named to commemorate the recovery of Henry VIII's flagship from the bottom of The Solent, the channel between the Isle of Wight and the southern coast of Britain. The ship was named for Mary Rose Tudor, Henry's sister.

HYBRIDIZER: David Austin
SUITABILITY: all levels
AVAILABILITY: wide
STATURE & HABIT: 5 feet ×
  5 feet (warm climate); 4 feet
  × 4 feet (cool climate)
FRAGRANCE: light

USES: tall shrub, border,
  cutting
PARENTAGE: 'Wife of Bath' ×
  'The Miller'
DISEASES: mildew, rust
DENOMINATION: AUSmary

Mary Rose

MARY WEBB

[*1984*]

A hidden gem among the English Roses, 'Mary Webb' is much overlooked, but in her own quiet way she is just as alluring as any of her flashier sisters.

Globular yellow-and-red buds open to very deep, cupped, 5- to 6-inch, soft lemony white blooms that fade to creamy white. The blooms carry a lovely soft lemony fragrance as well. New growth is bronze colored, and the seven-leaflet foliage is light green, round, and shiny. Canes are polished green with tiny needlelike red prickles. The robust and upright-growing shrub grows taller than it does wide. Hard pruning seems to encourage better repeat bloom. The half-open flowers are very deeply cupped to spheroid, and very graceful.

Try planting 'Mary Webb' in a grouping of three plants, placed closer than you would usually plant roses, for a huge color impact.

This cultivar is named for Mary Gladys Webb, a Shropshire novelist and poet who lived not far from the Austin nursery.

HYBRIDIZER: David Austin
SUITABILITY: all levels
AVAILABILITY: limited
STATURE & HABIT: 3 feet ×
   4 feet (warm climate);
   4 feet × 3 feet (cool climate)
FRAGRANCE: strong lemon

USES: border, cutting
PARENTAGE: seedling ×
   'Chinatown'
DISEASES: mildew, rust
DENOMINATION: AUSwebb

Mary Webb

MOONBEAM

[*1983*]

By no means a showy cultivar, this soft and subtle rose is easily overlooked. Growing 4 to 5 feet tall and somewhat wider, 'Moonbeam' is one of the more controllable English Roses.

Long, elegantly pointed peach-apricot buds unfurl to 4- to 5-inch, semi-double white flowers with tones of peach and apricot and prominent golden stamens. Flowers are produced in clusters on long stems, and the repeat bloom is dependable. Like the soft coloring, the fragrance is a subtle confection. New growth is edged with red and the foliage has a gray-green cast with green prickles. Mildew and black spot can be a problem, so be primed for occasional battles.

When in bloom, which is most of the time, 'Moonbeam' is best used to brighten up a dreary corner of the garden. Austin seems to prefer the fuller-petaled English Roses and has debated with himself over the course of time whether or not to retain the single and semi-double roses in this class. For me, there is no question of exclusion because there were and are many of this flower type among the Old Garden Roses. To banish these cultivars would be like ignoring what came before, and trying to rewrite history. Let's hope we get to see more like 'Moonbeam.'

HYBRIDIZER: David Austin

SUITABILITY: all levels

AVAILABILITY: limited

STATURE & HABIT: 5 feet ×
5 feet (warm climate);
3½ feet × 3 feet (cool
climate)

FRAGRANCE: light musk

USES: border, cutting

PARENTAGE: unknown

DISEASES: mildew, black spot

DENOMINATION: AUSbeam

Moonbeam

OTHELLO

[*1986*]

'Othello' is one of the top five or six most popular English Roses, and deservedly so. This tall shrub can be used as a freestanding bush or low climber, and the large flowers and prevailing perfume qualify it as an outstanding garden rose. The color will be much darker in cooler weather. After seeing this rose in a coastal garden, I realized that the almost-black red blooms were much happier in cooler weather that more closely resembled that of England than they were in my hotter inland garden.

Big orbs of buds open to corpulent 4- to 5-inch flowers. The petals curl back at the edges, creating large, open, very full reddish purple flowers with an underlying tone of yellow. The edges and reverse of the petals are a lighter, silver-pink tone. The fragrance is strong and fruity. New growth is light green and bronze, and the green canes are protected by an arsenal of red prickles. Repeat bloom is quite good, although sometimes a little more sparse in the hottest weather. The seven-leaflet foliage is dark green, contrasting beautifully with the color of the blossoms. Rust and mildew can be a bother at times, but with some protection, this is a completely dependable rose.

'Othello' is another superb candidate for self-pegging; in smaller gardens, you may want to try training it to an arbor, on a fence, or over a wall. The individual flowers are held on strong, upright stems and last well when cut at the half-open stage. All things considered, this is a most useful and desirable addition to the garden.

This rose is named after the tragic Moor, Othello, in Shakespeare's famous play.

HYBRIDIZER: David Austin
SUITABILITY: all levels
AVAILABILITY: wide
STATURE & HABIT: 6 to 8 feet × 5 feet (warm climate); 4 feet × 3½ feet (cool climate)
FRAGRANCE: strong and fruity

USES: tall shrub, climber, cutting
PARENTAGE: 'Lilian Austin' × 'The Squire'
DISEASES: mildew, rust
DENOMINATION: AUSlo
PATENT: 7213

Othello

PAT AUSTIN

[*1995*]

This is the first Austin rose to dip its head into more Promethean fires, for David Austin has historically sought coloration in keeping with the old-fashioned nature of his flower shape. She is on her way, but it will be a few years before 'Pat Austin' is widely available in this country. Believe me when I say the reward will be worth the wait.

Clusters of pointed orange-and-yellow buds open to elegant, 5- to 6-inch, shallow-cupped, semi-double flowers that are orange with yellow on the reverse. The petals cup inward but open up just enough to allow a glimpse of the red-tipped yellow stamens. The color has the same effect in the garden as 'Austrian Copper.' The strongly colored blooms have a lovely Tea Rose fragrance. The blooms age to a soft pink tone with a yellow base and paler reverse. New growth is shiny green with bronze edges, and the canes are purple-bronze with a polished, mahoganylike smoothness. The cardinal prickles are irregularly scattered, with some canes heavily covered with prickles and others almost thornless.

A rose of this intense coloration is going to be a surprise to growers who are used to the softer tones of English Roses. But what garden couldn't use a rose of a zesty hue to liven it up here and there?

'Pat Austin' is named for David Austin's wife, who is an accomplished sculptress.

HYBRIDIZER: David Austin
SUITABILITY: all levels
AVAILABILITY: limited
STATURE & HABIT: 4 to 6 feet × 4 feet (warm climate); 4 feet × 3½ feet (cool climate)
FRAGRANCE: Tea Rose

USES: border, cutting
PARENTAGE: unlisted
DISEASE: black spot
DENOMINATION: AUSmum
PATENT: applied for

Pat Austin

PEACH BLOSSOM

[*1990*]

Selecting a site for this most ephemeral of English Roses is a delicate matter. 'Peach Blossom' will grow tall if left on its own, but the translucent, semi-double blossoms deserve to be presented to their best advantage, which seems to be with backlighting. Think about placing this lovely cultivar so that the late afternoon sun, streaming through the garden, lights up the opalescent flowers, making it look like each one of them has its own tiny, self-contained lamp. Get a little lazy, forget to deadhead, and you will be rewarded with a sensuous crop of hips in the fall.

Clusters of long, pointed yellow-apricot buds open to semi-double, iridescent flowers of pale pink with yellow centers and bright golden stamens. As they age, the ruffled and notched blooms fade to the palest white-pink, and then to vanilla white. A sweet musky perfume completes the picture. Individual flower life is as brief as a breeze, but the reward comes in the nearly continuous bloom once the bush is established. New growth is reddish bronze, and the foliage is dark green and large with hordes of light green prickles. The tall shrub does get some mildew, although it's not really much of a worry.

This rose will tolerate light shade but will probably not bloom quite as frequently as it would when placed in more sun. Having grown 'Peach Blossom' both with and without support, I can say that when trained to a tall tripod or similar structure, this cultivar makes one of the strongest and loveliest statements of any English Rose.

This rose is so named because its flowers are remarkably similar to those of a peach tree.

HYBRIDIZER: David Austin
SUITABILITY: all levels
AVAILABILITY: mail order
STATURE & HABIT: 6 to 8 feet × 6 feet (warm climate); 4 feet × 3 feet (cool climate)
FRAGRANCE: sweet musk

USES: tall shrub, pillar
PARENTAGE: 'The Prioress' × 'Mary Rose'
DISEASE: mildew
DENOMINATION: AUSblossom

Peach Blossom

PEGASUS

[*1995*]

'Pegasus' has the look of 'Dove,' with the same Tea-like, pointed buds and open growth that spills out from the center. Austin describes this cultivar as low growing, but already in its first season, the new canes have shot up to almost 6 feet! This is another of the newer English Roses that may take a while to become readily available in this country.

Huge terminal clusters of fifteen buds or more, which unfurl with ribbed edges, open to 3½-inch, domed rosette-shaped yellow-and-apricot flowers with orange-apricot centers. The fragrance is very strong and Tea-like, carrying a hint of tobacco. The blooms fade to yellow with white guard petals. The strong dark green and bronze new growth is highlighted by the polished mahogany canes with large, hooked ruby prickles. Mature foliage is dark green, large, and oblong. Protect against mildew and black spot in areas with those problems.

There is an exceptional charm to 'Pegasus,' with its contrasting large yellow-and-apricot blooms and burnished mahogany canes. Cut flowers last well in bouquets.

Pegasus, the winged horse of Greek mythology, rose from the blood of the Gorgon Medusa after Perseus slew her.

HYBRIDIZER: David Austin
SUITABILITY: all levels
AVAILABILITY: limited
STATURE & HABIT: 5 to 6 feet
   × 5 feet (warm climate);
   3 feet × 3½ feet (cool climate)
FRAGRANCE: Tea-like

USES: border, cutting
PARENTAGE: unlisted
DISEASES: mildew, black spot
DENOMINATION: AUSmoon

Pegasus

PERDITA

[*1983*]

This is one of the English Roses that take their own perversely sweet time to establish. Its growth at first is very open and spreading, and only after three or four years does the empty center of the shrub begin to fill in. From the first bud, though, charming blooms of an exquisitely capricious nature progress through stages of almost ephemeral beauty. It's hard to imagine that the transitory progression of flowers is from the same plant. In fact, I use this rose to illustrate the point that it can be difficult to identify a rose from just one flower. When shown slides of the bud—the half-opened and the fully opened flower in succession—audience members are always astounded that the photographs were all taken of the same plant on the same day. But that is 'Perdita.'

Tea Rose-like, pointed, buff cream buds are produced in grand clusters. The blooms open to cupped, fully petaled flowers with soft peach centers waning to buttermilk white outer petals. The flower centers age to buff cream with time. At times in warmer weather, the color can have strong overtones of an orangy apricot. The new leaf growth is a spring green color and the canes come in bronze, mantled with both small and large red prickles. The foliage ages dark green, grows to substantial size, and can have some problem with rust and black spot. The flowers give off a strong Tea Rose perfume, and the plant repeats well.

'Perdita' has remained a very controllable 3 to 4 feet in size, but she is quite capable of growing to 7 feet or so if that is what your garden can accommodate. It is truly a most versatile shrub.

Perdita was the daughter of the king of Sicilia in Shakespeare's *The Winter's Tale.*

HYBRIDIZER: David Austin
SUITABILITY: all levels
AVAILABILITY: mail order
STATURE & HABIT: 3 feet × 3 feet (warm climate); 3½ feet × 3½ feet (cool climate)
FRAGRANCE: spicy Tea Rose

USES: border, cutting, partial shade
PARENTAGE: 'The Friar' × (seedling × 'Iceberg')
DISEASES: rust, black spot
DENOMINATION: AUSperd

Perdita

POTTER & MOORE

[*1988*]

One hates to say so, but this is another of those "you pays your money and you takes your chances" roses. The earliest flowers are almost always disfigured by balling, and the bush is inordinately prone to mildew and rust. However, with time and some extra tender loving care, this rose's unique charms can be coaxed to the fore and enjoyed. There is a distinct Old Rose character to the flowers, which to my eye have the distinct look of the Bourbon Rose.

Bulging pink buds open to fully petaled, cupped carnation pink blooms. Dark pink centers are shadowy while the reflexed, curled outer petals are almost white. The blooms carry a mild and sweet fragrance. The new growth is edged with bronze, and the seven-leaflet adult foliage ages a dark green with pinlike red prickles. The rebloom is good and the flowers are produced both individually and in small clusters. In warmer climates, the best flowers have been produced in the dry weather of summer and early fall.

Recently, while showing a renowned Old Rose expert around my garden, he literally flew over to this cultivar (which was covered with mildew and rust at the time, the flowers all balled and gray with fungus) and demanded to know from where I had collected this "great Old Rose!" The plant did look like it had to be a true Old Rose—I hated to tell him it was a new Austin introduction. It should be reiterated, however, that 'Potter & Moore' really does improve with a few seasons under its roots. It may also do much better in a hotter climate zone.

The name commemorates the introduction of a range of rose toiletries by the firm of Potter & Moore.

HYBRIDIZER: David Austin
SUITABILITY: intermediate
AVAILABILITY: mail order
STATURE & HABIT: 4 feet ×
   2 feet (warm climate); 4 feet
   × 3½ feet (cool climate)
FRAGRANCE: mild and sweet

USES: border, cutting
PARENTAGE: seedling of 'Wife
   of Bath'
DISEASES: mildew, black spot,
   rust
DENOMINATION: AUSpot

Potter
&
Moore

PRETTY JESSICA

[*1983*]

J ust because this is an exceedingly dependable rose doesn't mean that it is ordinary and common. Gardeners often seem to overlook the "dependables" among flowering plants in favor of seeking out the most difficult cultivars for their "unique" personal collections. For those merely searching for one of the best of the English Roses, 'Pretty Jessica' produces lovely blooms constantly and never grows over 3 feet tall. This is a great rose for the small garden, although it will show off most effectively if planted in groups of three or more. Try it in a container on the patio for almost continuous color and cut flowers.

Bright pink, pointed oval buds open to deeply cupped, 2½-inch vivid pink flowers with a strong honey-sweet fragrance. The outer, pale pink petals curl back and reflex to form a frame for the darker inner petals. Almost thornless, the canes are blanketed with large, oval, medium green foliage, which will need some protection from mildew and rust. 'Pretty Jessica' will produce a compact, low- but upright-growing shrub with good rebloom.

Jessica was the daughter of Shylock in *The Merchant of Venice.*

HYBRIDIZER: David Austin

SUITABILITY: all levels

AVAILABILITY: mail order

STATURE & HABIT: 3 feet × 2 feet (warm climate); 2½ feet × 2 feet (cool climate)

FRAGRANCE: sweet

USES: border, container, cutting

PARENTAGE: 'Wife of Bath' × seedling

DISEASES: mildew, rust, black spot

DENOMINATION: AUSjess

Pretty Jessica

PROSPERO

[*1982*]

A great rose for small gardens, 'Prospero' carries the unmistakable flower form and shrub qualities of the classic Gallicas on a truly modern, repeat-blooming shrub. The small garden simply cries out for the likes of this cultivar, and whether planted in a container or used as a low hedge, 'Prospero' has all the charm of the great Old Roses of yesteryear.

Globular scarlet buds have a unique, flat, cut-off look to the half-open bloom. Flowers open flat and then reflex back to form a pompon. The dusky red petals are ruffled and crimped with pointed ends smudged with black tones. Produced in large, open clusters, the flowers age to black-red with strong purple tones, and they emit a brawny, candied fragrance. The color change from red to purple is very pleasing and true to the old-fashioned style of the flower form. Large, jungle green foliage envelops the shrub, and the canes are defended by tough, needle-like red-and-green prickles.

Mauve and purple roses went out of vogue back with the changeover from candlelight and gaslight to modern electric lights. Good purple-tone roses are few and far between these days, and it is nice to find one that's not only a reliable rose but also comes on a low-growing, sturdy bush.

This rose is named after the rightful duke of Milan in Shakespeare's *The Tempest,* who was deposed by his brother and the king of Naples and cast adrift at sea along with his daughter, Miranda. They eventually land on a mysterious island, and Prospero becomes a student and scholar of the magic arts.

HYBRIDIZER: David Austin
SUITABILITY: all levels
AVAILABILITY: mail order
STATURE & HABIT: 3 feet ×
  4 feet (warm climate);
  4 feet × 3 feet (cool climate)
FRAGRANCE: strong and sweet

USES: low hedge, container,
  border
PARENTAGE: 'The Knight' ×
  'Château de Clos Vougeot'
DISEASES: mildew, rust
DENOMINATION: AUSpero

Prospero

PROUD TITANIA

[*1983*]

This cultivar is not without its problems. The flowers almost always ball in spring, they are slow to repeat, and the plant has been very prone to mildew and rust, even in a fairly dry climate. The flowers are always wonderfully too numerous to count, but they are consistently spoiled by balling and mildew in the cool, damp weather of spring. Later in the year, with the driest weather, the problems diminish but are never quite eradicated. 'Proud Titania' might fare best if you live in a very hot, very dry climate zone.

Huge, spherical, cream-colored buds open to flat, fully petaled rosettes that are creamy white with a hint of pale apricot blush and pink. The outer petals are notched and the centers sport a button eye that completely hides the stamens. The dark green foliage is also prone to disease, so protection will again be necessary in cool and damp climate zones. The tall, upright-growing canes are sheathed with prickles of many sizes. The Damask-like flowers have a sweet rosy fragrance, and their form does improve with the arrival of warmer weather. Repeat bloom also improves with age but can still be somewhat erratic.

'Proud Titania' has, for all intents and purposes, been superseded by much more dependable English Roses. In truth, however, the charming flowers and otherwise robust nature of this cultivar do justify a place for her in the right garden. After all, one of the prime reasons for growing English Roses is their old-fashioned nature—and this one has that character description with plenty to spare.

Titania was the queen of the fairies and wife of Oberon in Shakespeare's *A Midsummer Night's Dream.*

HYBRIDIZER: David Austin
SUITABILITY: intermediate
AVAILABILITY: limited
STATURE & HABIT: 6 feet ×
   6 feet (warm climate); 4 to
   5 feet × 4 feet (cool climate)
FRAGRANCE: sweet

USES: tall shrub, climber,
   self-pegging
PARENTAGE: seedling × seedling
DISEASES: mildew, rust
DENOMINATION: AUStania

Proud Titania

REDCOAT

[*1973*]

I f blood red roses are your thing, this is the one for you. A sanguine grenadier standing to attention with aplomb, 'Redcoat' simply will not be ignored in the garden.

Cone-shaped scarlet buds are produced in phenomenally prolific clusters, sometimes reaching thirty or more flowers at a time. The five-petaled, 4-inch, scarlet-crimson flowers open freely, displaying a central yellow eye with striking yellow-gold stamens. As the shrub matures, it develops into an inverted cone shape, much wider than tall. This 6-foot-tall-plus sentinel drapes itself with shiny dark green foliage and lancets of prickles. 'Redcoat' can be cut back but seems to want to grow tall again before reblooming.

This is one of the English Roses better suited to hotter climate zones. The more subtle tones of the 'Redcoat' sport 'Dappled Dawn' may prove superior in some old-fashioned gardens, but 'Redcoat' is a large, robust shrub that will make quite a statement if placed in the garden with thoughtful consideration. It seems to work best if situated as a freestanding shrub in its own corner; otherwise, it may crowd out any close neighbors. Another option might be to try stationing a pair of these scarlet-clad sentries on guard near a formal entrance to your garden. The effect will be quite striking and bold, and what garden couldn't use a fusillade of intense color to welcome visitors.

Once you see the blooms on the 'Redcoat' bush, you will understand the name.

HYBRIDIZER: David Austin
SUITABILITY: all levels
AVAILABILITY: mail order
STATURE & HABIT: 6 to 8 feet
  × 6 feet (warm climate); 5 to
  6 feet × 5 feet (cool climate)
FRAGRANCE: light

USES: tall shrub, hedge
PARENTAGE: 'Parade' × seedling
DISEASES: none of note
DENOMINATION: AUScoat

Redcoat

REDOUTÉ

[1992]

Except for its color, this plant grows and produces flowers identical to 'Mary Rose,' from which it sported. Like that cultivar, 'Redouté' can take its time to establish. One could wonder, why another pink rose? But 'Mary Rose' is such an excellent cultivar that she tends to pass on her charming nature to all her children.

'Redouté' is in every way the same as 'Mary Rose' except that the flowers are a softer shade of pink. In fact, the very Damask nature of this shrub extends to the way it holds its healthy green foliage and twiggy canes cloaked with fine prickles. Even the leaves are folded along the center rib, much as its ancient predecessors.

Don't be too surprised if you find white or bright pink flowers mixed in with the softer pink roses on 'Redouté.' From time to time, you can find a number of plants sporting back to both 'Mary Rose' and 'Winchester Cathedral' in the local garden center. Not a bad idea, getting three roses for the price of one.

This cultivar is named for the French "Raphael of flowers," Pierre-Joseph Redouté (1759–1840), who was the court painter of flowers to Empress Josephine. Redouté illustrated one of the most important early rose books, *Les Roses.*

HYBRIDIZER: David Austin
SUITABILITY: all levels
AVAILABILITY: limited
STATURE & HABIT: 5 feet ×
  4 feet (warm climate);
  4 feet × 4 feet (cool climate)
FRAGRANCE: light

USE: border, cutting
PARENTAGE: sport of 'Mary
  Rose'
DISEASE: mildew
DENOMINATION: AUSpale
PATENT: 8789

Redouté

ST. CECILIA

[*1987*]

O ne could search long and hard among Modern Roses and only come up with half the charm and purity of the old-fashioned roses that this English Rose displays. The soft blush pink blossoms have a feminine charm, yet the robust growth gives the shrub a curiously masculine edge. 'St. Cecilia' decked out with bloom is reminiscent of a Coco Chanel creation: no bows, no frills—a simple, urbane, tailored suit of a rose.

Round red buds produce large, 3- to 4½-inch, deeply cupped pale blush flowers that hold their shape throughout their lives. The scent is a mix of rose and myrrh. Flowers are produced mostly one-to-a-stem, with an occasional cluster. New growth is green with a bronze-colored reverse, and the canes are light green with tiny red prickles; otherwise, the new canes are smooth. As the canes age, the thorns turn red-brown, and there are five to seven long, pointed leaflets to a stem. A medium to tall shrub, 'St. Cecilia' tends to be upright, so self-pegging might help encourage more repeat bloom. This cultivar will accept hard pruning, allowing you to keep it to about 4 feet. Although mildew can be a problem, a dose of the standard prevention will cure it easily.

St. Cecilia, the patron saint of musicians, is usually depicted playing a musical instrument and wearing a wreath of roses.

HYBRIDIZER: David Austin
SUITABILITY: all levels
AVAILABILITY: wide
STATURE & HABIT: 6 feet ×
   3 feet (warm climate);
   3 feet × 2 feet (cool climate)
FRAGRANCE: strong myrrh

USES: border, hedge, cutting
PARENTAGE: 'Wife of Bath' ×
   seedling
DISEASES: mildew, rust
DENOMINATION: AUSmit
PATENT: 8157

St. Cecilia

ST. SWITHUN

[*1993*]

'St. Swithun' should come with a warning: Beware. Climber ahead! The Austin catalog describes this new cultivar as being a vigorous, bushy shrub of 3 feet with good disease-resistance, but in this country, it consistently sends out immense, arching canes to 8 feet and higher. Not a rose for the front of the border, obviously.

Positively obese carmine buds with paler highlights open to 3½-inch, shallow-cupped flowers. The blush pink blooms are enlivened with a hint of golden apricot, and the flower centers form a classic button eye. The outer petals are much lighter and the scent has a strong myrrh perfume. The flowers are never perfectly round in outline but almost scalloped, and the tight knot of petals forming the central button eye is so tight as to remind one of a chignon. New growth is edged in bronze, and the foliage is dark green with seven leaflets. Canes are covered with red-tipped green prickles, which age to a brown-red. Flowers are produced in terminal clusters on long, billowing canes that can easily reach 8 feet. The repeat bloom can be a bit sparse, at least until the shrub is well established. Plant 'St. Swithun' so that it spills over a wall, casting its myrrh scent into the garden path for your visitors.

St. Swithun was the bishop of Winchester from A.D. 852 to 862. According to the legend, if it rains on July 15th, St. Swithun's Day, it will rain for 40 days and 40 nights afterward. This cultivar was named by Austin to commemorate the 900th anniversary of the founding of Winchester Cathedral.

HYBRIDIZER: David Austin
SUITABILITY: all levels
AVAILABILITY: limited
STATURE & HABIT: 6 feet ×
   8 feet (warm climate);
   3½ feet × 3 feet (cool climate)
FRAGRANCE: strong myrrh

USE: large shrub, cutting
PARENTAGE: 'Mary Rose' ×
   ('Chaucer' × 'Conrad
   Ferdinand Meyer')
DISEASE: mildew
DENOMINATION: AUSwith
PATENT: 9010

St. Swithun

SHARIFA ASMA

[*1989*]

Only recently has 'Sharifa Asma' become readily available in this country. A delicate, low-growing shrub, this cultivar lends itself to being planted as a hedge of six to eight bushes or in groups of three as a focal point in the garden. 'Sharifa Asma' is reminiscent of one of its parents, 'Admired Miranda,' but unlike that rose, this one seems to possess just a bit more vigor in both growth and repeat bloom.

Yellow-carmine buds open to 3-inch cupped flowers that continue to reflex until they end up as flat rosettes. Ruffled, pale shell pink outer petals surround neatly quartered, button-eyed centers of peachy apricot tones, while the guard petals are much paler. The delicate inner petals exhale a scrumptious bouquet of Old Rose. Petals possess an inner luminosity that warms each bloom from within. New growth has a burnt ocher patina, and the canes are mossy green clothed with small, triangular red prickles. Mature leaves are a dark matte green and quite rugose. The low-growing shrub has, so far, bloomed continuously, even through the hottest summer.

'Sharifa Asma' will need some time to settle into a garden, often taking two to three years to develop a sturdier frame, so it will require a good deal of patience and regular doses of tender loving care. As a start, a deep mulch with organic compost or manure 2 to 3 inches deep will make the shrub very happy. In addition, regular applications of a timed-release fertilizer alternated with fish emulsion, as well as regular irrigation, will go a long way toward promoting healthy growth.

If you plan to cut flowers from 'Sharifa Asma,' make sure to plant at least three bushes. This will ensure a steady supply of fragrant blooms for even the most demanding flower arranger.

The right to name this rose was purchased by a private party in the United Kingdom.

HYBRIDIZER: David Austin
SUITABILITY: all levels
AVAILABILITY: wide
STATURE & HABIT: 4 feet ×
   3 feet (warm climate);
   3 feet × 2 feet (cool climate)
FRAGRANCE: strong rose

USES: border, low hedge,
   container, cutting
PARENTAGE: 'Mary Rose' ×
   'Admired Miranda'
DISEASE: black spot
DENOMINATION: AUSreef
PATENT: 8143

Sharifa Asma

SHROPSHIRE LASS

[*1968*]

'Shropshire Lass' is every bit a modern form of the classic Alba Rose, which should be no surprise as the Old Hybrid Alba 'Mme. Legras de St. Germain' is one of her parents. Another characteristic shared with her Alba ancestors is a tolerance for shade. This cultivar will be quite happy to grow and flower in areas where other roses would turn up their roots and give up the ghost. Give it room and stand back. There have been reports of 'Shropshire Lass' growing to 15 feet in Connecticut! For me, she easily attained 12 feet in the first season after planting, and so was replanted in a site appropriate for a large, freestanding specimen. This shrub is only once-flowering, in the spring, but worth it where the space is available.

Elegantly pointed, brownish pink-toned buds open to 4-inch, single-petaled, blush pink shields of flowers with just a hint of yellow and a central boss of delicate flaxen stamens. The blooms fade to white with age. Other characteristics passed from the Alba parent are her long, feathery sepals and very fine prickles extending right out to the calix— all of which add to the strong Old Garden Rose charm of the shrub. The flowers drop well when finished, so you will not have to deadhead, and the round hips will add interest and color to the fall garden. Blue-green foliage, which ages deep green, and canes well stocked with scythelike red prickles finish off this exuberant shrub.

Plant 'Shropshire Lass' as a tall hedge along a long, curving drive-way or walkway, or use her to create a partition with which to divide two garden rooms. She can even be planted as a single specimen at the back of the border. There seems to be strong reticence on the part of many gardeners to give up precious garden space to once-flowering roses, but any garden can benefit from the intense spring display and the fall color these roses provide.

Shropshire is one of England's most picturesque and beautiful pas-toral districts, located near the Austin nursery.

HYBRIDIZER: David Austin
SUITABILITY: all levels
AVAILABILITY: limited
STATURE & HABIT: 12 feet ×
    10 feet (warm climate);
    8 feet × 6 feet (cool climate)
FRAGRANCE: mild

USES: tall shrub, back of
    border, hedge, climber
PARENTAGE: 'Mme. Butterfly' ×
    'Mme. Legras de St.
    Germain'
DISEASES: none of note
DENOMINATION: none

*Shropshire
Lass*

SIR CLOUGH

[*1983*]

E ven in our colder climes, this cultivar's reputation for growing tall and very thorny will be well met, attaining heights of 5 feet or more. In warmer zones, the vaulting canes reach out to 8 feet and longer, making it a difficult rose to place in many gardens. 'Sir Clough' will tolerate hard pruning, although self-pegging will definitely come in handy to keep this one under control.

Rings of hot pink buds, produced in large, terminal clusters of up to nine, open to 4-inch, shallow-cupped, semi-double cerise pink flowers with prominent clumps of gold stamens. There is a hint of yellow at the base of the petals. New growth is green with bronze on the reverse of the leaves. The fragrance is strong of Old Roses, and lushly sweet. This robust cultivar has good, clean foliage and the rebloom is excellent. Stop deadheading in the fall if you want a crop of large hips.

In my garden, this rose has been trained onto a tripod made by tying together three 8-foot garden stakes and wrapping the pliant canes around the structure. Once the canes are bent over, they break into bloom at every node all along the stems, and the flowers are then produced in bewildering numbers. Every third year or so, remove the old, spent canes and tie the best of the new canes back around the tripod. This system creates some height in an otherwise level garden and allows you to grow an ungainly shrub in a limited space. Not only do you get a great display of flowers in spring, but crops of bloom grace the garden throughout the season.

Austin compares the flower of this cultivar to 'Apothecary's Rose' (*Rosa gallica officinalis*), but in truth, there is a decidedly modern feel to 'Sir Clough.' The name may be a problem for us on this side of the Atlantic (it rhymes with "rough"), but this is one of the more interesting English Roses. For those with the space and patience to do some training, this is an exceptional choice.

This cultivar is named for Sir Clough Williams-Ellis (1883–1978), the architect and designer of Portmeirion Village in North Wales.

HYBRIDIZER: David Austin
SUITABILITY: all levels
AVAILABILITY: mail order
STATURE & HABIT: 8 feet ×
  5 feet (warm climate);
  5 feet × 3 feet (cool climate)
FRAGRANCE: strong Old Rose

USES: tall shrub, climber,
  cutting
PARENTAGE: 'Chaucer' ×
  'Conrad Ferdinand Meyer'
DISEASES: none of note
DENOMINATION: none

Sir
Clough

SIR EDWARD ELGAR

[*1992*]

If there were a rose that could fit the description "a horse of a different color," this could just be the one. Neither red nor pink, 'Sir Edward Elgar' seems as though its blooms are lit from underneath in order to light the way through the garden.

Burgundy red oval buds open to 4-inch, fully petaled, ruffled cerise-carnelian flowers with a silvery reverse. Blooms are produced in clusters of three to four and have a lightly honeyed scent. The sometimes quartered flowers reflex back quite a bit, giving the blooms the look of peonies resting on the low to medium-tall bush. The bright cerise of the flowers is softened to a whitewashed pink as the blooms age. Repeat bloom is very good, and the color blends very well with many perennials. New growth is green with a red edge, and small red prickles cover the light green canes. The dark green foliage covers the plant well but does have some problem with mildew.

Austin describes this cultivar as growing to about 3 feet, but it tends to grow a little larger here in the States. Plant this one in groups of two or three for an abundant display of lustrous bloom.

This cultivar is named in honor of the English composer Sir Edward Elgar (1857–1934).

HYBRIDIZER: David Austin
SUITABILITY: all levels
AVAILABILITY: limited
STATURE & HABIT: 5 feet ×
    5 feet (warm climate);
    3½ feet × 2 feet (cool climate)
FRAGRANCE: mild

USES: border, container,
    cutting
PARENTAGE: 'Mary Rose' ×
    'The Squire'
DISEASES: mildew, rust
DENOMINATION: AUSprima
PATENT: 8670

*Sir Edward
Elgar*

SIR WALTER RALEIGH

[*1985*]

This cultivar walks a thin red line between a good rose and one not quite worth taking up garden space. 'Sir Walter Raleigh' can grow to 6 feet or more, but the flowers, although large and sweet, are not always produced with quite the abandon one could hope for in an English Rose. However, there is a certain Gallica-like charm to this rose, with its rugose foliage and armory of light brown prickles.

Large, 4-inch, deeply cupped, semi-double flowers open from round red buds. The strongly fragrant blooms are a glorious warm carnation pink with paler reflexes that open to display a central knob of canary-colored stamens. The flower shape is not unlike that of a tree peony on a tall, upright-growing, tough shrub. Flowers are produced in clusters of three to four. Repeat bloom is only so-so in nature, and mildew and rust can be a problem in some areas of the country. New growth is reddish, aging to textured dark green, seven-leaflet foliage. The canes have a peculiar zigzag pattern to their growth. Like Gallicas, the bushes of 'Sir Walter Raleigh' may spread around the garden when planted on their own roots, so it is wise to give each plant some growing space.

The name commemorates the 400th anniversary of the first English colony in America on Roanoke Island. Sir Walter Raleigh (1554–1618), the founder of the settlement, was a favorite of Elizabeth I.

HYBRIDIZER: David Austin
SUITABILITY: intermediate
AVAILABILITY: limited
STATURE & HABIT: 6 feet ×
  3 feet (warm climate);
  4 feet × 3 feet (cool climate)
FRAGRANCE: strong Old Rose

USES: tall shrub, hedge
PARENTAGE: 'Lilian Austin' ×
  'Chaucer'
DISEASES: mildew, rust
DENOMINATION: AUSspry
PATENT: 7213

Sir Walter Raleigh

SWAN

[*1987*]

Good white roses are few and far between. In light of the fact that 'Iceberg' is one of this cultivar's parents, one would have hoped for a much better shrub. For one thing, the rust in spring is just overwhelming; so if rust is a particular problem in your area, it would be wise to start early with preventives or steer clear of it altogether. On top of this, like many white roses, the flowers are often spoiled by brown streaks and edges—telltale evidence of a thrips infestation. Thrips live and feed inside buds, causing their damage to the opening flowers.

Traditionally shaped, Hybrid Tea-like, butter yellow buds open to flat-topped, buff white flowers that soon reflex back to tight rosettes packed with short crimped-and-ruffled petals. The 2½- to 3-inch flowers, produced in large clusters, are only lightly scented. In cool weather, 'Swan' produces buff yellow flowers that soon fade to pure white. The new growth is green with bronze on the reverse, and the tall, straight canes are smooth with scattered light green prickles and dark green foliage. 'Swan' is a tall, robust-growing shrub that can be kept to 4 or 5 feet tall with hard pruning.

'Swan' does have her faults, but she produces a consistently astounding bounty of bloom and can be a wonderful addition to any garden.

This cultivar was named for the swanlike purity and grace of its white flowers.

HYBRIDIZER: David Austin
SUITABILITY: intermediate
AVAILABILITY: mail order
STATURE & HABIT: 6 feet ×
   5 feet (warm climate);
   5 feet × 5 feet (cool climate)
FRAGRANCE: light

USES: border, tall shrub,
   cutting, partial shade
PARENTAGE: 'Charles Austin' ×
   (seedling × 'Iceberg')
DISEASE: rust
DENOMINATION: AUSwhite
PATENT: 7564

Swan

SWEET JULIET

[*1989*]

For such a large-growing shrub, the flowers are unfortunately a bit small. In recent seasons, though, 'Sweet Juliet' has begun to improve. She does seem to need high culture: a deep, organic mulch of 2 to 3 inches; regular applications of fertilizers; and regular, deep irrigation. Austin waxes lyrical on the fine qualities of the long, pointed foliage, but in the States, that same foliage seems almost always to be spoiled by mildew early in the year. It may fare better in the hot, dry climate zones of the Southwest.

Small yellow-apricot buds open to 2-inch, shallow-cupped, peachy apricot flowers with a heady, fruity, Tea Rose fragrance. New growth is bronzed, and the canes are light green and smooth with ruby red prickles. When not malformed by mildew, the leaflets are produced in sets of seven and are light green in color. A tall shrub, this plant will attain 6 to 8 feet, so self-pegging might be in order.

This cultivar and 'Jayne Austin' are two of Austin's favorites. In fact, 'Sweet Juliet' is one of the most popular of the English Roses in the entire United Kingdom. All reports give her the highest marks over there. Juliet is, of course, the cherished daughter of the Capulets in *Romeo and Juliet.*

HYBRIDIZER: David Austin
SUITABILITY: all levels
AVAILABILITY: wide
STATURE & HABIT: 6 feet ×
   4 feet (warm climate);
   4 feet × 3 feet (cool climate)
FRAGRANCE: fruity, Tea Rose

USES: tall shrub, climber
PARENTAGE: 'Graham Thomas'
   × 'Admired Miranda'
DISEASE: mildew
DENOMINATION: AUSleap
PATENT: 8153

Sweet Juliet

TAMORA

[*1983*]

'Tamora' packs all the best qualities of the Old Garden Roses into a compact shrub that just doesn't stop blooming. This is the most Gallica-like and, by far, one of the best English Roses introduced to date, due to the quality and quantity of blooms, the fragrance, and the diverse amount of color, which is truly phenomenal. 'Tamora' has only recently become available in this country, but she will repay the gardener who takes the time and trouble to hunt for her with armloads of fragrant flowers.

Bright orange-red bud spheres open to 3½-inch, deeply cupped, heavenly myrrh-scented orange-peach-apricot blooms, produced either in large clusters or one to a stem. The new growth is bronze, and canes are a polished café noir color. The seven-leaflet, dark green rugose foliage creates a marvelous background for the mass of flowers. Canes are cloaked with red-bronze stiletto-like prickles. Growth is low and upright with the flowers produced on long stems for cutting.

Hardly ever out of bloom, 'Tamora' is best planted en masse. In my garden, she is planted in a bed of over sixty roses in two crescent-shaped beds around the front of the Temple of Love, a beautiful, re-stored, seventeeth-century limestone *tempietto*. At the height of bloom, the perfume can be inhaled from the far side of the garden! Sited at the head of the rose garden, the *tempietto* and beds of 'Tamora' have become so popular for photographers that the walkway becomes impassable on weekends.

Tamora was the queen of the Goths in Shakespeare's *Titus Andronicus*—and not a lady to take lightly.

HYBRIDIZER: David Austin
SUITABILITY: all levels
AVAILABILITY: mail order
STATURE & HABIT: 3½ feet ×
   2½ feet (warm climate);
   3 feet × 2 feet (cool climate)
FRAGRANCE: strong myrrh

USES: border, container, hedge,
   cutting
PARENTAGE: 'Chaucer' ×
   'Conrad Ferdinand Meyer'
DISEASE: rust
DENOMINATION: AUStamora

Tamora

THE ALEXANDRA ROSE

[*1992*]

A departure from the usual English Roses, this cultivar has the look of the Alba class from which it receives much of its charm. The billowing long canes and gray-green foliage with silver reverse also point to a relationship with the Albas.

Buds are produced in large clusters at the ends of the lengthy, curving canes. Peg or self-peg the canes so they will respond by producing shorter flowering stems all along their length. Buds are pointed and very Alba-like with their ornamental, long, foliate sepals. The yellow to orange buds unfurl to 2½-inch, five-petaled flowers of a delicious shade of coppery pink with a yellow eye and gold stamens. Prominent red-gold stigmas round off the flowers, which tend to fade quickly through shades of pink to end up white. Repeat bloom is frequent and dependable. New growth is green edged in bronze, and the young canes are polished bronze with a few scattered green prickles. Mature foliage is gray-green, long, and pointed, and generally made up of seven-leaflet sets. Hips manifest themselves in prodigious quantities and can be very decorative in the fall.

'The Alexandra Rose' can take time to develop, so don't despair. It will eventually produce vaulting canes that can reach out to 8 feet or so. This is another large shrub that will make a lovely freestanding specimen, or you can try arching it over and self-pegging to keep it within bounds. One might even try using it as a low climber trained over a garden arch or cascading over a wall. As 'The Alexandra Rose' has a good dose of Alba in its background, it just might tolerate more shade than many of the other cultivars.

The name commemorates Queen Alexandra (1844–1925), wife of Edward VII and founder of the Alexandra Rose Day charity in the United Kingdom.

HYBRIDIZER: David Austin
SUITABILITY: all levels
AVAILABILITY: limited
STATURE & HABIT: 6 feet × 5 feet (warm climate); 4½ feet × 4 feet (cool climate)
FRAGRANCE: light

USES: tall shrub, climber, partial shade
PARENTAGE: ('Shropshire Lass' × 'Shropshire lass') × 'Heritage'
DISEASES: none of note
DENOMINATION: AUSday

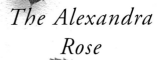

The Alexandra Rose

THE COUNTRYMAN

[*1987*]

It has taken some time to realize just how good a rose this cultivar is. 'The Countryman' has received a strong dose of the OGRs from its Portland parent, 'Comte de Chambord.' Take a close look at the willowy canes covered with prickles, the dark green foliage folded up along the midribs, the blossoms, themselves glorious pompons blanketing the entire plant; sniff the Damask scent. There is an atavistic force at work here—'Comte de Chambord' in disguise!

Clear pink, 3-inch flowers are produced from rounded, deep pink buds with long, foliate sepals. The quartered flowers open to domed rosettes revealing golden yellow tints at the center with a strong Old Rose perfume. New growth is penciled in bronze, mature foliage is dark forest green with a bright gray reverse, and leaflets are typically folded up along the center rib. The canes are covered with light green prickles of mixed sizes, which age to a red-brown. 'The Countryman' has good resistance to disease. If not deadheaded, the round hips will create a lovely fall display.

This rose will need support for the weak, lax canes so that the plant doesn't become too floppy. You have two basic optimal-plant-size choices. With hard pruning, 'The Countryman' makes a good, solid, low shrub with dependable bloom. If you decide to keep it tall or long, as with many taller plants, self-pegging seems to be the best answer; trained in this manner, the plant will perform much better with multiple flowering cycles. Another trick you may want to try, which will render roughly the same growth size as self-pegging, is to allow the canes to grow to 6 feet or so, then tie them to a stake at about two-thirds their height so you get an upright shrub that cascades down from the top in the manner of a cascading tree rose. This is a very striking, effective look, and the repeat bloom thus produced is phenomenal.

'The Countryman' is named for a popular British magazine.

HYBRIDIZER: David Austin
SUITABILITY: all levels
AVAILABILITY: limited
STATURE & HABIT: 6 feet ×
  6 feet (warm climate);
  3 feet × 2 feet (cool climate)
FRAGRANCE: strong Damask

USES: tall shrub, low climber,
  tree rose, self-pegging
PARENTAGE: 'Lilian Austin' ×
  'Comte de Chambord'
DISEASE: mildew
DENOMINATION: AUSman
PATENT: 7556

The
Countryman

THE DARK LADY

[*1991*]

The dusky crimson blooms of 'The Dark Lady' as described for the United Kingdom seldom live up to the name on this side of the Atlantic. In our hot summers, the flowers unfold to more of a medium pink, sometimes darker, and then fade quickly. With cooler weather, the dark tones do improve.

Orbs of reddish pink buds open to very full, 4-inch, deep pink to red flowers with a silver reverse and a central button eye. The outer petals curve down, forming a petticoat effect. The flowers have a strong Old Rose fragrance. New growth is light green with red edges, maturing to pointed, shiny hunter green foliage. Canes are pale green with reddish prickles. Regular deadheading will encourage rebloom and help prevent cane dieback. If mildew is a problem in your area, an ounce of prevention will help this cultivar along.

Austin likens the flowers of 'The Dark Lady' to tree peonies. The bush is low growing and a bit wider than tall. This is one of those cultivars that can take a few years to settle into the garden, but give it the time and the tender loving care it needs, and it will repay your trouble with wonderfully fragrant blooms.

'The Dark Lady' is named for the famed mystery lady of William Shakespeare's sonnets.

HYBRIDIZER: David Austin
SUITABILITY: all levels
AVAILABILITY: limited
STATURE & HABIT: 3 feet ×
  4 feet (warm climate);
  3 feet × 3½ feet (cool climate)
FRAGRANCE: strong Old Rose

USES: border, container,
  cutting
PARENTAGE: 'Mary Rose' ×
  'Prospero'
DISEASES: mildew, rust
DENOMINATION: AUSbloom
PATENT: 8677

The Dark Lady

THE FRIAR

[*1969*]

'The Friar' is a rose for the collector who wants as many unusual English Roses as possible in the garden. Like some of his other early introductions, Austin no longer lists this cultivar in his catalog and it has been difficult to acquire. The main interest in 'The Friar' is that it was used to breed 'Admired Miranda'; like that rose, it tends to lack vigor and takes several years to settle into the garden. The plant I received was small and rather slow to grow, but over time it has established itself nicely.

Pointed orange-apricot, Tea-like buds open to semi-double, 3½-inch, strongly fragrant pale apricot-buff flowers. New growth is bronze and the mature foliage dark green with red prickles. The plant is low growing, weak, and subject to dieback.

This is a shrub that really requires "high culture": great attention to disease prevention, a 2- to 3-inch-deep organic mulch, and regular attention to irrigation and fertilizing. All this and no promise that the rose will repay the effort with flowers.

Chaucer's Friar was a "limiter," or a begging friar, who had purchased a district to beg in.

HYBRIDIZER: David Austin
SUITABILITY: advanced
AVAILABILITY: limited
STATURE & HABIT: 2 feet ×
  2 feet (warm climate);
  4 feet × 3 feet (cool climate)
FRAGRANCE: strong and spicy

USES: border, container
PARENTAGE: 'Ivory Fashion' ×
  seedling
DISEASES: mildew, black spot
DENOMINATION: none

The Friar

THE HERBALIST

[*1991*]

Can't surrender precious garden space to a rose that only blooms in spring? Then this is the English Rose for you! One of the most interesting of the newer Austin cultivars, 'The Herbalist' looks like it could have been lifted directly from a cloister garden.

Deep pink, semi-double, 3-inch flowers open from round red buds. Ruffled petals open up just enough to display a centered boss of golden stamens and red pistils. New growth is light green edged with red. 'The Herbalist' grows nicely upright on light green canes armed with numerous red-tipped prickles. The dark green foliage has good resistance to disease. But the best characteristic this cultivar possesses is its propensity to bloom—it seems never to be out of flower. The fragrance is light and rosy.

Plant 'The Herbalist' in clusters of three plants to take advantage of the cultivar's naturally upright nature and blooming power. Such a planting maximizes the impact the rose will have in the garden and provides an almost continuous display of bloom. Stop deadheading in the fall and you will be presented with a crop of fine red hips to extend the garden interest of the shrub well into winter.

'The Herbalist' is very Gallica-like; in fact, Austin named it because of its striking similarity to the 'Apothecary's Rose,' also known as *Rosa gallica officinalis,* a classic rose of truly ancient origin. Plants given the Latin title *officinalis* were used for herbal medicines by doctors and pharmacists.

HYBRIDIZER: David Austin
SUITABILITY: all levels
AVAILABILITY: mail order
STATURE & HABIT: 4 feet ×
   3 feet (warm climate);
   3 feet × 3 feet (cool climate)
FRAGRANCE: light

USES: border, low hedge,
   container
PARENTAGE: seedling × 'Louise
   Odier'
DISEASE: mildew
DENOMINATION: AUSsemi

The Herbalist

THE KNIGHT

[*1969*]

'The Knight' is one of David Austin's earliest creations, and it has clearly been superseded by many of his later and greater introductions. This staunch warhorse is a rose for the collector or connoisseur who just must have it because of the name and its position as the first of the repeat-blooming red English Roses. The reported parentage is 'Chianti' crossed with an English Rose seedling, and 'Chianti' itself is the product of a cross between the dark red, single-flowered Floribunda 'Dusky Maiden' and the great red Gallica 'Tuscany.' 'The Knight' has good dose of the Old Rose about it. This English Rose has been difficult to obtain in this country without an import permit from Europe, but recently at least one mail-order source has made it available.

Red buds open to 3-inch medium-red to cerise flowers, which are produced in small clusters. The petals reflex back to form domed pompon-shaped flowers with a rich, Damask-like fragrance. New growth is green tinted bronze with triangular red prickles and large, oval foliage. So far, the bush is low and somewhat weak growing, but given some time, it will probably reach 3 feet in height.

This weak cultivar will require some extra tender loving care: a 3-inch mulching with organic compost, regular applications of fertilizer, constant attention to water, and regular deadheading.

Chaucer's Knight was a courteous gentleman who was honored for his chivalry; his tale was one of honor and unrequited love.

HYBRIDIZER: David Austin
SUITABILITY: connoisseur
AVAILABILITY: limited
STATURE & HABIT: 3 feet ×
  2 feet (warm climate);
  3 feet × 2 feet (cool climate)
FRAGRANCE: Damask Rose

USES: border, container,
  cutting
PARENTAGE: 'Chianti' ×
  seedling
DISEASES: mildew, rust
DENOMINATION: none

The Knight

THE NUN

[*1987*]

There is a lovely, soft quality to 'The Nun.' The individual flowers have a tulip-like essence that sets it apart from other white English Roses. The shrub grows in an open manner, wider than tall, and will take a few years' growth to fill in.

Exquisite, Tea-like, pointed buff white buds open to elegant, cupped, semi-double blush white blooms with red-gold stamens at the center. The 2½-inch flowers are produced in large clusters and give off a sweet honey-myrrh fragrance. The tulip quality is enhanced by the fact that the blooms don't open out of the cup, but hold their shape as they age to white. The foliage is dark green on green canes with red prickles. The open nature of the plant is further emphasized by the sparse but healthy foliage. Though modest in nature, 'The Nun' repeats well. If not deadheaded, this cultivar, like most single and semi-double roses, will set a good fall crop of decorative hips.

This cultivar is named for the nun from Geoffrey Chaucer's *The Canterbury Tales,* where she is listed as the Second Nun. Her contribution to the travelers' entertainment is the tale of St. Cecilia.

HYBRIDIZER: David Austin
SUITABILITY: all levels
AVAILABILITY: limited
STATURE & HABIT: 6 feet ×
   6 feet (warm climate);
   4 feet × 3 feet (cool climate)
FRAGRANCE: honey-myrrh

USES: border, tall shrub
PARENTAGE: 'The Prioress' ×
   seedling
DISEASE: mildew
DENOMINATION: AUSnun

The Nun

THE PILGRIM

[*1991*]

Although in the United Kingdom 'The Pilgrim' is a somewhat more modest shrub, once established in the American garden, it can attain a height of 8 feet or more.

Round, mottled red-yellow buds are produced in large clusters of up to twenty. The 3-inch flowers open to flat-topped, quartered rosettes with bright yellow center petals that fade to pale yellow-white guard petals. The sun can pull the yellow color right out of this one, though. Often in the hottest weather, the flowers will fade to white in a matter of hours. The fragrance is that of a mild Tea Rose. The tall, upright light green canes come packaged with shiny, healthy, seven-leaflet holly green foliage and large, triangular garnet-and-jade prickles.

'The Pilgrim' is an upright grower to around 6 feet, and while the canes continue to grow, they begin to arch outward, reaching 10 feet or more in the time from August to late September. The bud eyes are not always placed right at the joint, or axil, of the leaf but are sometimes sited between the leaves. Although the bloom color will probably stabilize in cooler weather and climates, in hot weather the flowers are smaller in size and very similar to 'Yellow Button.' So far, the repeat is intermittent; again, this will improve with age and the passage of seasons.

Even though 'The Pilgrim' is a robust shrub, pruning back after each flowering cycle will help control the bush to a more reasonable garden size. Don't be surprised if your first-year plant blooms only for a short while. Given a season or two of growing, 'The Pilgrim' will put on a good continuous show well into late summer, when even the mature plant will take time off from flowering and decide to stage a late surge of growth. Train this cultivar over an arch, allow it to tumble over a wall, or self-peg the bush not only to control the ultimate size but also to promote more bloom throughout the season.

HYBRIDIZER: David Austin
SUITABILITY: intermediate
AVAILABILITY: wide
STATURE & HABIT: 6 to 8 feet or more × 6 feet (warm climate); 5 feet × 4 feet (cool climate)
FRAGRANCE: spicy Tea Rose

USES: tall shrub, climber, cutting
PARENTAGE: 'Graham Thomas' × 'Yellow Button'
DISEASE: mildew
DENOMINATION: AUSwalker
PATENT: 8678

The Pilgrim

THE PRINCE

[*1990*]

'The Prince' is the darkest tone of crimson purple so far introduced among the English Roses. It harks back to the purple roses of the eighteenth and nineteenth centuries. There is no hint of the metallic lilac tones of modern mauve-colored roses. This royal rose possesses the noticeably atavistic charm of the long-lost Bourbon or Gallica Roses of yesteryear.

At the half-open stage, the buds are globe shaped, dark red with darker red-black markings. The flowers eventually open to slightly domed, flat rosettes of the darkest red-purple and black. This color is marked with iridescent tones of hot pink on the inner petals and black-red on the outer guard petals. New growth is dark bronze and the mature foliage dark green with small red prickles. The foliage will need some protection from mildew in damp climates. So far, 'The Prince' has grown to around 3 feet and may get just a bit taller; it does not have the vigor of some of the other English Roses, but with time it will settle into the garden. The fragrance is a wonderful Old Rose, Damask-like scent that can't help but add to the old-fashioned appeal of this cultivar. Repeat bloom, even though a bit slow, is dependable.

Through the last 150 years, roses of this color were often given names that included the word *prince.* It is thought that this Prince remembers Edward, the Black Prince of England, who defeated the French at Poitiers in 1356, thus securing a rich wine-growing district for the English crown.

HYBRIDIZER: David Austin
SUITABILITY: intermediate
AVAILABILITY: wide
STATURE & HABIT: 3 feet ×
   4 feet (warm climate);
   2½ feet × 3 feet (cool
   climate)
FRAGRANCE: strong Old Rose

USES: border, container,
   cutting
PARENTAGE: 'Lilian Austin' ×
   'The Squire'
DISEASES: mildew, black spot,
   rust
DENOMINATION: AUSvelvet
PATENT: 8813

The Prince

THE PRIORESS

[*1969*]

Not listed in many compendiums these days, 'The Prioress' is one of the better white English Roses from the early days of Austin's breeding program. Often overlooked, white roses are useful to brighten up dark garden corners or, in situations where night lighting is available, to simply glow and bring the garden alive at dusk or in the moonlight.

Round, buffy cream buds open to fragrant, 3-inch, semi-double, blush pink to white flowers with gold stamens and red pistils. New growth is light green edged red, and the mature, disease-resistant foliage is dark green held on green canes with red prickles. The fragrance is a mix of Tea Rose and spice. A tall, lusty shrub, 'The Prioress' has a strong, upright growth habit. 'Ma Perkins,' one of the listed parents, is an uncommon Floribunda that one doesn't see much of these days.

This rose is named after Chaucer's Prioress, whose motto was *Amor vincit omnia,* or "love conquers all." No stranger to courtly manners, she dipped her food just so into the sauce so as to never muss her fingertips, and wiped her upper lip so clean that not a trace of grease was seen upon her cup.

HYBRIDIZER: David Austin

SUITABILITY: all levels

AVAILABILITY: limited

STATURE & HABIT: 6 feet ×
   6 feet (warm climate);
   4 feet × 4 feet (cool climate)

FRAGRANCE: spicy Tea Rose

USES: tall shrub, hedge

PARENTAGE: 'Ma Perkins' ×
   seedling

DISEASE: mildew

DENOMINATION: none

The Prioress

THE REEVE

[*1979*]

A picture of 'The Reeve' in a Los Angeles garden column was instrumental in raising public awareness of English Roses. Although a number of collectors had been growing these roses for some time, the Austins hadn't made it into garden centers and national catalogs. Then articles in the media created such a demand that nurseries were forced to hunt high and low to find growers to supply the demand. Still one of the best of the Austin roses, 'The Reeve' has a truly heavenly fragrance.

Red to hot pink buds open to cupped, 3½-inch, scalloped, bright pink petals. The petals of the globe-shaped blooms pull back just enough to reveal a glimpse of red-gold stamens at their center. The petal reverse is silver-pink, occasionally striped with paler pink. New growth is bronze, shouldering bright red prickles, and the foliage is a shiny malachite green. Clusters of blooms nod on the ends of slender stems. The fragrance is strong and musky, reminding one of the classic Old Roses. The repeat bloom is good, but the plant growth habit is open and somewhat susceptible to mildew.

Although superseded by newer, stronger-growing English Roses, 'The Reeve' seems to define just what Austin was after when he began hybridizing this class: fragrance, repeat bloom, growth habit, and old-fashioned charm of flower.

In Chaucer's time, a reeve was an official of the manor who oversaw the discharge of feudal obligations.

HYBRIDIZER: David Austin
SUITABILITY: all levels
AVAILABILITY: mail order
STATURE & HABIT: 5 feet ×
   4 feet (warm climate);
   4 feet × 4 feet (cool climate)
FRAGRANCE: strong and musky

USES: border, mass planting,
   cutting
PARENTAGE: 'Lilian Austin' ×
   'Chaucer'
DISEASES: mildew, black spot
DENOMINATION: AUSreeve

The Reeve

THE SQUIRE

[*1977*]

Everyone is still searching for the perfect red rose. We want it to be dependably reblooming, essentially disease-resistant, and long lasting as a cut flower, with a wonderful, heady perfume. Sadly, such a rose doesn't exist and quite possibly never will. 'The Squire,' although not a contender for the first rank, does come in with strong perfume, good rebloom, and a wonderful Old Rose charm.

This rose likes to strut its stuff. Fat, dark red buds open to deeply cupped, 4½-inch flowers of the deepest velvet crimson with the petals often edged in coal-red, bordering on black, as the flower matures. They are full and long lasting, both on the bush and as a cut flower. But it is the fragrance that catches the attention, a heady, Old Rose perfume that imprints in the memory of anyone who ever sticks his or her nose into a bloom. Dark green foliage and red prickles are added attractions that set off the flowers to perfection. The plant grows to an upright 4 feet, which lends itself to groupings of three bushes closely planted for maximum color and effect. The rebloom, once the plant is established, is superb and dependable.

With all the work that goes into creating new red roses each year, 'The Squire' is still one of the best dark red English Roses when grown in the right part of the country. It needs heat and sun to ward off its propensity to mildew, and requires some extra protection from this problem in areas that have summer rain and humidity; in the drier parts of the country, this rose is prone to the malady only in early spring and late fall. Try some of the newer, less toxic controls for mildew, like the new super-refined oils or fungicidal soaps, and see if they don't help.

Chaucer was an astute observer of the human condition and used his skill to describe his times. His Squire was a dandy who spent most of his time concerned with his appearance and attire; singing and playing the flute all day, he would have blended right into the London Court Chaucer knew all too well.

HYBRIDIZER: David Austin
SUITABILITY: all levels
AVAILABILITY: wide
STATURE & HABIT: 4 feet ×
   3 feet (warm climate);
   4 feet × 4 feet (cool climate)
FRAGRANCE: strong Old Rose

USES: border, low hedge,
   container, cutting
PARENTAGE: 'The Knight' ×
   'Château de Clos Vougeot'
DISEASE: mildew
DENOMINATION: AUSsquire

The Squire

THE YEOMAN

[*1969*]

I have called this rose every name in the book. The flowers can be spectacular and carry a heavenly fragrance, but it is a poor grower that is far too prone to mildew and rust. This is a rose for someone who will take the time to really give it the *best* cultivation. It does tend to improve with age, however.

Pink and yellow-apricot buds open to 3-inch, flat, quartered flowers of the palest pink-apricot tint that possess an indescribable, sweet myrrh fragrance. New growth is bronze and the round, foresty green foliage contrasts well with the flowers. Once established, 'The Yeoman' has a dependable repeat bloom. The foliage is prone to most problems, so it will be necessary to step in with preventive sprays. The plant is also prone to considerable dieback, but regular removal of spent blooms will help control this problem.

The plant is low growing, so it would be best in the front of a sunny border. Plant two or three in a cluster to gain maximum flower production. Tender loving care will go a long way in helping this cultivar overcome its problems with disease and lack of vigor. Deep mulching with a rich organic compost, regular care in irrigation and fertilizing, and attention to disease prevention is what this rose requires.

Chaucer's Yeoman served the Knight, and Chaucer describes him as a proper forester, clad in a cloak and hood of green. A good English yeoman should be hardy and stalwart, not requiring coddling. But if you love fragrance and have a warm, sunny spot in your garden and a soft spot in your heart, this rose will repay you with some of the loveliest and most intensely perfumed blooms imaginable.

HYBRIDIZER: David Austin
SUITABILITY: advanced
AVAILABILITY: limited
STATURE & HABIT: 3 feet ×
2 feet (warm climate);
3 feet × 2 feet (cool climate)
FRAGRANCE: strong myrrh

USES: front of border,
container, cutting
PARENTAGE: 'Constance Spry' ×
'Monique'
DISEASES: mildew, black spot,
rust
DENOMINATION: AUSyeo

*The
Yeoman*

TRADESCANT

[*1993*]

'Tradescant' is a relatively new introduction of very limited availability in this country, but it is one to put on your list for future choice garden additions.

Flat-topped, black-red buds are produced in large open clusters of ten to fifteen buds, which open to 2½- to 3-inch, fully petaled, velvety-textured burgundy, red, and purple flowers that are edged and mottled with black. Blooms are packed with small, quill-shaped petals that fill the flower, allowing only a few yellow stamens to peek out here and there. They emit an elysian perfume of Old Rose. The flowers age to almost pure velvet black with wine red, pointed petal tips. New growth is deep green outlined in red. The large, oval, hunter green foliage is healthy to the extreme. Light green canes are well armed with plentiful emerald prickles. 'Tradescant' is a robust shrub, growing to 4 or 5 feet and then arching outward to 8 feet or more.

This cultivar is named in honor of the Tradescant Trust, which is building the Museum of Garden History on the site of the historic church of St. Mary-at-Lambeth, London. The Tradescants—John the Elder (circa 1570–1638) and John the Younger (1608–1662)—were gardeners and naturalists in Jacobean England.

HYBRIDIZER: David Austin
SUITABILITY: all levels
AVAILABILITY: limited
STATURE & HABIT: 6 to 8 feet × 6 feet (warm climate); 2 feet × 2½ feet (cool climate)
FRAGRANCE: strong Old Rose

USES: border, tall shrub, climber, cutting
PARENTAGE: 'Prospero' × ('Charles Austin' × 'Gloire de Ducher')
DISEASES: none of note
DENOMINATION: AUSdir
PATENT: 9009

Tradescant

TREVOR GRIFFITHS

[*1994*]

Pink roses are available to such an extent that a few years back a major rose company in this country decided not to introduce any new roses of this color. But still, pink is definitely a popular color when one thinks of roses. The problem is in wading through all of those available to find the few truly good cultivars for the garden. 'Trevor Griffiths' has good possibilities, with its Old Rose charm and fragrance.

Pointed pale pink buds with darker edges open to large (3- to 4-inch), shallow-cupped, dusky pink flowers with lighter edges. As the flowers open, they take on a flat shape that is added to by the confusion of petals, giving the blooms a distinctive, old-fashioned, Damask-like look. The flowers give off a lovely, Damask-like Old Rose perfume. New growth is celadon green brushed with bronze, and the canes are antiqued umber with multitudes of small red prickles attached. The mature foliage is textured into a dark green, making a lovely contrast to the flowers. If you live in a region where black spot can be a problem, you will need to protect this cultivar against the disease.

It is a little early to say just how tall 'Trevor Griffiths' will grow, but indications are that it will be in the 3- to 5-foot range with a slightly wider spread.

The real-life Trevor Griffiths is a nurseryman and author from New Zealand's South Island, who has helped to popularize Old Roses through his catalogs and books.

HYBRIDIZER: David Austin
SUITABILITY: all levels
AVAILABILITY: limited
STATURE & HABIT: 3 to 5 feet
× 4 feet (warm climate);
3½ feet to 4 feet × 3 feet
(cool climate)
FRAGRANCE: sweet Old Rose

USES: border, container,
cutting
PARENTAGE: unlisted
DISEASE: black spot
DENOMINATION: AUSold

Trevor
Griffiths

TROILUS

[*1983*]

With all of this cultivar's problems, you could ask why one would bother growing it. An answer might be for the wonderful honey and myrrh fragrance. But be forewarned: This is another English Rose that needs a great deal of tender loving care. Deep organic mulching, frequent deadheading to prevent dieback, and regular irrigation will help, but don't forget to use something to prevent disease. This is definitely not a rose for the beginner, but one to tackle after cutting your teeth on some of the easier cultivars.

Tulip-like buff yellow buds open to deeply cupped, 3-inch, honey buff to apricot pink flowers with just a hint of yellow at the center. Flowers open out of the cupped form with pointed and ruffled petals. Matte green foliage and scarlet prickles thrive on a spindly plant, which tends to be very stingy with its repeat bloom. The plant will improve with age, but it still is not overly generous with bloom. Mildew, black spot, and rust can all be a predicament for this rose.

A difficult cultivar to grow, 'Troilus' will eventually settle into the garden, given time and care.

This rose is named after a title character in Shakespeare's play *Troilus and Cressida*. The son of King Priam of Troy, Troilus loved Cressida, who betrayed him by becoming the mistress of the handsome Greek Diomedes.

HYBRIDIZER: David Austin
SUITABILITY: advanced
AVAILABILITY: limited
STATURE & HABIT: 2 feet × 2 feet (warm climate); 4 feet × 4 feet (cool climate)
FRAGRANCE: honey-myrrh

USES: border, container
PARENTAGE: ('Duchesse de Montebello' × 'Chaucer') × 'Charles Austin'
DISEASES: mildew, black spot, rust
DENOMINATION: AUSoil

Troilus

WARWICK CASTLE

[*1986*]

'Warwick Castle' is another of those "difficult to place" English Roses that demand just the right spot in the garden. Best when used as a ground cover in this country, the 3-foot shrub does occasionally throw out long, billowing canes that will spill out to 6 feet or more. Flowers are produced in good quantities in warm, dry weather. The old-fashioned nature of bloom is only enhanced by the accompanying enchantingly heady perfume.

Round bright carmine buds with large, decorative sepals open to domed, fully petaled, warm pink flowers with a button eye. These rest atop a low shrub with lax, arching canes. New growth is edged with bronze, and the hunter green oval foliage, when free of mildew, creates a fine background for the flowers. Early in the season, with the damper weather, the flowers almost always ball; this rose is very prone to rust, so very few good flowers are produced until the hotter weather sets in. 'Warwick Castle' can seem to be a slave to its problems, but when conditions are optimal, it can be a truly outstanding plant.

The growth of this cultivar is very much like that of its parent, 'Lilian Austin,' which gives 'Warwick Castle' its inclination to be used as a low-growing, wide-spreading ground cover.

This rose commemorates the opening of the Victorian rose garden at Warwick Castle.

HYBRIDIZER: David Austin

SUITABILITY: intermediate

AVAILABILITY: limited

STATURE & HABIT: 3 feet ×
6 feet (warm climate);
3 feet × 3 feet (cool climate)

FRAGRANCE: strong

USES: border, ground cover

PARENTAGE: 'Lilian Austin' ×
'The Reeve'

DISEASES: mildew, rust

DENOMINATION: AUSlian

Warwick
Castle

WENLOCK

[*1984*]

Even though 'Wenlock' can't be listed among the top English Roses, there may yet be a place in the garden for this fragrant, robust-growing red cultivar. When in bloom, it always elicits notice from garden visitors. A tall, lusty shrub, the plant is very thorny, and the foliage has good resistance to mildew. Other than the fact that there were few Gallica Roses of this coloration, there is something very Old Rose-like about this cultivar.

Clusters of rotund, bright red buds open to 3-inch, cupped, medium-crimson to purple flowers. The large and sweetly fragrant flowers are nicely clustered, and the bloom repeats reasonably well. Seven-leaflet, light green new growth is edged with red, and the canes are covered with a multitude of crimson prickles, giving this cultivar a decidedly Gallica-like look. If not deadheaded later in the season, 'Wenlock' will produce a large crop of round red hips in the fall. The plant is tall and a strong grower, often reaching 6 feet and more; self-pegging will help control the shrub as it increases the repeat bloom. Some protection against black spot will be necessary.

This cultivar is named for a limestone ridge in Shropshire, Wenlock Edge, which is mentioned in "The Welsh Marches," a poem by A. E. Housman.

HYBRIDIZER: David Austin
SUITABILITY: all levels
AVAILABILITY: mail order
STATURE & HABIT: 6 to 10 feet
  × 6 feet (warm climate);
  5 feet × 5 feet (cool climate)
FRAGRANCE: strong and sweet

USES: tall shrub, climber
PARENTAGE: 'The Knight' ×
  'Glastonbury'
DISEASE: black spot
DENOMINATION: AUSwen

Wenlock

WIFE OF BATH

[*1969*]

A mong the earliest of the English Roses, 'Wife of Bath' is still one of the most popular, and rightly so. Its strong constitution and fragrance mark this cultivar as truly unforgettable as her namesake. The flower color and low-growing habit place her among the English Roses possessing a strong affinity to the Old Gallica Roses of the eighteenth century.

Carnation pink oval buds open to 3-inch, shallow-cupped, bright clear pink flowers with bashful blush pink centers. The petals have a notch in them and recurve back, giving an elegant poise to the blooms, with just a glimpse of golden stamens at the center, much like one of the parents, 'Mme. Caroline Testout.' The charm of the bloom is enhanced by a hearty, sweet fragrance of myrrh. New growth is chestnut with seven-leaflet, forest green foliage and canes covered with carnelian red prickles. 'Wife of Bath' may need some protection from mildew in damp climates, although this disease has not proven to be much of a problem in the dry Southwest. The compact shrub has a strong and dependable repeat bloom. Occasionally subject to a little dieback, just prune out the offending deadwood to keep her going.

Chaucer's Wife of Bath was hardly demure. She saw five husbands to the church door and was widely traveled, having made pilgrimages to Jerusalem, Rome, and the shrine of St. James Compostella in Spain.

HYBRIDIZER: David Austin
SUITABILITY: all levels
AVAILABILITY: mail order
STATURE & HABIT: 4 feet ×
   3 feet (warm climate);
   4 feet × 3 feet (cool climate)
FRAGRANCE: strong myrrh

USES: border, hedge, cutting
PARENTAGE: 'Mme. Caroline
   Testout' × ('Ma Perkins' ×
   'Constance Spry')
DISEASE: mildew
DENOMINATION: AUSbath

Wife of Bath

WILD FLOWER

[*1986*]

As noted, David Austin has been increasingly reluctant to include the five-petaled, single form within the category English Roses. For him, it seems only the fully petaled, double roses can genuinely represent the classic Old Rose character. True, most Old Roses surviving today are fully doubled flowers, but there were, and still are, classic single-flowered roses that are without question Old Roses.

'Wild Flower' is just such an example: a wonderful, strong single rose exhibiting all the character of the most cherished five-petaled Old Roses. It represents an inextricable link between Austin's English Roses and the centuries-old singles that, admittedly or not, his work emulates.

Clusters of pointed yellow buds flourish on a large, wide-spreading plant that will need plenty of room to grow. The buds will open to single-petaled, soft pale yellow flowers that fade to white with just a hint of yellow at the petal base. The single-petaled form displays the bright golden stamens to perfection. Light green new growth is edged in bronze. Stop deadheading in September, and 'Wild Flower' will reward you by producing an excellent crop of round scarlet hips later in the fall. Although the individual flowers are only 2- to 3-inches across, they are produced in large clusters that cover the sweeping canes. The combination of those arching canes, along with the five-petaled flowers and large crop of oval hips, gives this shrub a true Wild Rose look. The flowers have a light Tea Rose-like scent. Canes are covered with brick red, needle-sharp prickles and matte green, seven-leaflet foliage carrying good resistance to disease. The plant is vigorous and will grow much wider than tall. The flowers age well and are not spotted with pink in cool or damp weather, unlike some other single yellow roses.

The choice of name is obvious, given the nature of this rose's Species-like look and wide-spreading growth. A charming addition to any garden.

HYBRIDIZER: David Austin
SUITABILITY: all levels
AVAILABILITY: limited
STATURE & HABIT: 5 feet ×
  7 feet (warm climate); 2 feet
  × 2½ feet (cool climate)
FRAGRANCE: light Tea Rose

USES: ground cover, low hedge,
  border
PARENTAGE: 'Canterbury' ×
  (seedling × 'Golden Wings')
DISEASE: mildew
DENOMINATION: AUSwing

Wild Flower

WILLIAM SHAKESPEARE

[*1987*]

In the cooler regions of the United States, 'William Shakespeare' will produce phenomenally large, fragrant flowers, while in the hotter regions, the flowers will be somewhat smaller in proportion to the tall, robust shrub. Give this rose a few years to settle into the garden, as he takes several seasons to produce the best growth and flowers.

Clusters of black-red buds open to dark red, 3½- to 4-inch, slightly domed, pompon-shaped flowers. The central petals curl inward to form a button eye and have cerise to red tones; the outer petals take on purple to black highlights. New growth is bronze with numerous large and small maroon prickles scattered along the canes. The fragrance matches the Old Garden Rose look of the flowers and shrub with a wonderful Damask-like scent. The deep jade green, textured, oval-shaped foliage will need protection from rust and black spot in damp climates. The repeat bloom is good. From time to time, this cultivar will produce a flower with what looks like a notch cut out of the side of the bloom, which gives a kidney shape to the open flower. This is attributed to too many petals in the bud, which causes the calix to split. Not that much of a problem, but the defect is aesthetically noticeable.

'William Shakespeare' is one of those roses you want to love just because of the name. Placed at the rear of the border, or mixed in with lower-growing, pale-colored roses, the flat, deep maroon blossoms add an air of antebellum charm to any rose border.

HYBRIDIZER: David Austin
SUITABILITY: all levels
AVAILABILITY: mail order
STATURE & HABIT: 6 feet ×
   3 feet (warm climate);
   4 feet × 3 feet (cool climate)
FRAGRANCE: strong Damask
   Rose

USES: tall shrub, hedge, cutting
PARENTAGE: 'The Squire' ×
   'Mary Rose'
DISEASES: rust, black spot
DENOMINATION: AUSrush

William Shakespeare

WINCHESTER CATHEDRAL

[*1988*]

'Winchester Cathedral' is a sport—the product of an accident—and not the result of the hybridizer's art. It has all the great points of its parent, 'Mary Rose,' but its crisp white flowers stand out brightly in the garden, making their own distinctive statement.

Globular buds open to clusters of 3-inch, notched and scalloped, snow white, very classically fragrant blossoms. In cool weather, like most other white roses, 'Winchester Cathedral' will take on cameo pink tones, but for the rest of the year it will be white. New growth is edged with a bronze ocher, maturing to dark green healthy foliage, while the canes are covered with pale prickles of mixed sizes. The shrub will take a few years to grow to its 5- to 6-foot-tall height. Like 'Mary Rose,' 'Winchester Cathedral' has the look of the Old Damask Roses, all packaged in a healthy, repeat-blooming shrub.

All the 'Mary Rose' sports have that Tudor exuberance and renaissance flair that only Henry VIII and his family could impart to their age. White is a color that gardeners in this country often overlook, but when used to highlight a darker garden space or to separate deep red or pink flowers, white can be most effective.

This rose was named in aid of the Winchester Cathedral Trust, which oversees the restoration and maintenance of the famous church.

HYBRIDIZER: David Austin
SUITABILITY: all levels
AVAILABILITY: wide
STATURE & HABIT: 6 feet ×
    5 feet (warm climate);
    4 feet × 4 feet (cool
    climate)
FRAGRANCE: light rose

USES: border, hedge, cutting
PARENTAGE: sport of 'Mary
    Rose'
DISEASE: mildew
DENOMINATION: AUScat
PATENT: 8141

*Winchester
Cathedral*

WINDRUSH

[*1984*]

Austin describes this rose as being an improvement on 'Golden Wings,' which is one of its parents. The lanky, sprawling growth of 'Windrush' does seem to hark back to that parent's Species Rose ancestry. This cultivar has a row or two more petals than its parent and does have dependable rebloom, but otherwise it retains little of the Old Rose look to gain it English Rose status.

Clusters of pointed maize-colored buds edged in pink open to lemon yellow, semi-double flowers with a display of prominent stamens at the centers. The fragrant blooms fade to white with age. Light green new growth matures to shiny holly green, healthy, pointed, seven-leaflet foliage that covers the shrub. The canes are well shielded by large, brier-like light red and yellow prickles. 'Windrush' is a large shrub, growing to 6 feet tall and 8 feet wide. Planted in a closely spaced row or group, this cultivar would make a great protective barrier or hedge to keep away intruders. The large, round hips are produced with abandon, so it will be necessary to deadhead on a regular schedule to encourage rebloom, only stopping in late September to ensure a festive crop of ornamental hips.

Plant this cultivar with enough room to take advantage of its large growth and plentiful bloom. Special attention to placement can add to its beauty as the pale yellow, semi-double flowers will take on an unearthly glow when backlit by the late afternoon sun.

HYBRIDIZER: David Austin
SUITABILITY: all levels
AVAILABILITY: mail order
STATURE & HABIT: 6 feet ×
   8 feet (warm climate);
   4 feet × 4 feet (cool climate)
FRAGRANCE: spicy

USES: tall shrub, hedge, back
   of border
PARENTAGE: seedling ×
   ('Canterbury' × 'Golden
   Wings')
DISEASE: mildew
DENOMINATION: AUSrush

Windrush

WISE PORTIA

[*1982*]

There are times in the garden when 'Wise Portia' can take on the look of a bush covered with anemones, as many of the stamens turn to black as the blooms age. At other times, this cultivar has all the charm of a Gallica Rose taken right out of Josephine's garden at Malmaison. Either way, the small shrub is notable as one of the best of the low-growing red English Roses.

Clusters of pointed cherry buds open to 3½-inch, shallow-cupped, carmine-red to purple blooms that reflex back to form rosette-shaped flowers with pointed and scalloped petals. The petals open just enough to display a hint of yellow stamens at the bloom center, and the flowers have a lovely, strong Old Rose scent. New growth is edged with red and the dark green, shiny, pointed foliage has good disease-resistance. The canes are protected with grass green thorns. The low-growing shrub is very dependable and always in bloom.

This Portia is named for the heroine of Shakespeare's *The Merchant of Venice.*

HYBRIDIZER: David Austin
SUITABILITY: all levels
AVAILABILITY: mail order
STATURE & HABIT: 3 feet ×
  4 feet (warm climate);
  2½ feet × 2½ feet (cool
  climate)
FRAGRANCE: strong Old Rose

USES: border, container,
  cutting, partial shade
PARENTAGE: 'The Knight' ×
  'Glastonbury'
DISEASES: mildew, black spot
DENOMINATION: AUSport

Wise Portia

YELLOW BUTTON

[*1975*]

Not all that old-fashioned looking, 'Yellow Button' could be, in reality, a Floribunda just as easily as an English Rose. The small flowers do have charm, and the compact-growing shrub does deserve a place in the border, but you will find it can hold its own among the most modern Floribundas or Hybrid Teas as easily as at the front of your Austin bed. Try planting a cluster of two or three to make a strong statement among some of the taller-growing cultivars.

Large clusters of round buds open to form rosettes of bright yellow, 2-inch flowers that are almost egg-yolk orange at the centers. The outer petals reflex back on themselves and fade to white. The color is ephemeral and fades rather quickly in hot sun, but in cool weather they hold their color. There is a light, fruity fragrance evoked from the petals, and the repeat bloom is quite good. New growth is light green and almost thornless. 'Yellow Button' covers itself with healthy, disease-resistant foliage.

Austin produced 'Yellow Button' from an unusual cross. One of its parents is the Floribunda 'Chinatown,' which can grow to over 10 feet in warm zones while remaining around 3 feet in the colder areas of the country. At times the flowers can look almost identical to the Noisette 'Alister Stella Gray,' but on a much lower-growing shrub. 'Yellow Button' is a nice shrub that is hardly ever out of bloom. There should be a place in any border for this solid, dependable English Rose.

HYBRIDIZER: David Austin
SUITABILITY: all levels
AVAILABILITY: limited
STATURE & HABIT: 3 feet ×
    4 feet (warm climate);
    3 feet × 3 feet (cool climate)
FRAGRANCE: light

USES: border, container
PARENTAGE: 'Wife of Bath' ×
    'Chinatown'
DISEASE: black spot
DENOMINATION: none

Yellow Button

YELLOW CHARLES AUSTIN

[*1981*]

Austin seems to prefer his original introduction, 'Charles Austin,' over the yellow sport of this large, vigorous plant. 'Yellow Charles Austin' has also been superseded by newer and better yellow English Roses. That said, there can be a place for this cultivar in the garden. The growth habit and flower form are the same as those of 'Charles Austin,' except that the flowers are a lemony yellow color. Like its apricot form, hard pruning right after each bloom cycle will keep the shrub at a lower, more manageable height, or you can use the self-pegging method to train the 10-foot canes as a shaped climber, which should encourage more rebloom and fill up an unused corner of the garden.

Large, fat reddish yellow buds open to 4-inch lemon yellow flowers that are fully petaled and reflex back to form a distinctive cup-shaped bloom. Vigorous new growth is green edged in maple red, and the large, mature foliage is an emerald green. The blooms have a fruity fragrance, and the repeat bloom can only be improved by cutting the canes back hard after each flowering cycle.

Simply allowing this cultivar to grow to any height will not produce much bloom, as the roses will grow to 10 feet or more and produce only a cluster of three blooms at the tops of the 10-foot canes. Training this rose along a fence is another good option, as it will improve the rebloom and turn a so-so cultivar into quite a dependable garden rose.

'Yellow Charles Austin' is the yellow-flowering sport of the apricot-pink 'Charles Austin,' which was named for David Austin's father.

HYBRIDIZER: David Austin
SUITABILITY: all levels
AVAILABILITY: limited
STATURE & HABIT: 10 feet ×
   6 feet (warm climate);
   5 feet × 5 feet (cool climate)
FRAGRANCE: strong and fruity

USES: tall shrub, climber
PARENTAGE: sport of 'Charles
   Austin'
DISEASES: mildew, black spot
DENOMINATION: AUSyel

*Yellow
Charles
Austin*

Appendix A

NORTH AMERICAN MAIL-ORDER SOURCES *for* ENGLISH ROSES

The retail and mail-order sources listed herein are for North America and all grow and offer English Roses for sale, among other classes of roses. These sources offer their own catalogs and ship roses at the appropiate season for your region of the country. Mail-order suppliers do have the advantage of offering a broad selection for your choosing. Well-packaged and shipped bare-root roses will grow and thrive if you take care and plant them as soon as possible.

During the spring, bare-root planting season, many local nurseries and garden centers offer a selection of English Roses for sale. Here, you have the advantage of being able to examine the canes and roots to make sure you are receiving a vigorous and healthy plant.

Gardeners living in the United States will not be able to order some cultivars of English Roses from the Canadian nurseries because Austin has exclusive contracts with the American nurseries, and patent and trademark laws prohibit Canadian nurseries from shipping certain cultivars into this country.

ARENA ROSE COMPANY
536 West Cambridge Avenue
Phoenix, AZ 85003-1007
PHONE: 602-266-2223
FAX: 602-266-4335
COLOR CATALOG: $5.00
✳ *Offers 60 cultivars of grafted English Roses*

HEIRLOOM OLD GARDEN ROSES
24062 Riverside Drive N.E.
St. Paul, OR 97137
PHONE: 503-538-1576
FAX: 503-538-5902
COLOR CATALOG: $5.00
✳ *Offers 90+ cultivars of own-root English Roses*

HORTICO, INC.
723 Robson Road, R.R. 1
Waterdown, Ontario L0R 2H1, Canada
PHONE: 905-689-6984
FAX: 905-689-6566
COLOR CATALOG: $3.00
✳ *Offers 90+ cultivars of grafted English Roses*

JACKSON & PERKINS CO.
One Rose Lane
Medford, OR 97501-0702
PHONE: 800-292-4769
FAX: 800-242-0329
COLOR CATALOG: free
✳ *Offers 11 cultivars of grafted English Roses (offerings will increase in next few years)*

PICKERING NURSERIES INC.
670 Kingston Road
Pickering, Ontario L1V 1A6, Canada
PHONE: 905-839-2111
FAX: 905-839-4807
COLOR CATALOG: $4.00
✳ *Offers 71 cultivars of grafted English Roses*

SMITH & HAWKEN
Two Arbor Lane
Florence, KY 41022-6900
PHONE: 800-776-3336
FAX: 606-727-1166
COLOR CATALOG: free
✳ *Offers a limited, very selective assortment of English Roses in spring*

WAYSIDE GARDENS
1 Garden Lane
Hodges, SC 29695-0001
PHONE: 800-845-1124
FAX: 800-457-9712
COLOR CATALOG: free
✳ *Offers 38+ cultivars of grafted English Roses*

Appendix B

LIST *of* PUBLIC GARDENS DISPLAYING ENGLISH ROSES *for* VIEWING

This is a guide to various gardens across the country that have— or plan to have—English Roses on display.

CALIFORNIA

DESCANSO GARDENS
1418 Descanso Drive
La Cañada-Flintridge, CA 91011
PHONE: 818-952-4400
HOURS: 9:00 A.M. to 4:30 P.M.

GARDEN VALLEY RANCH
498 Pepper Road
Petaluma, CA 94952
PHONE: 707-795-0919
HOURS: Wednesday through Sunday
10:00 A.M. to 4:00 P.M.

THE HUNTINGTON LIBRARY, ART COLLECTIONS, AND BOTANICAL GARDENS
1151 Oxford Road
San Marino, CA 91108
PHONE: 818-415-2141
HOURS: Tuesday through Friday
12:00 noon to 4:30 P.M.; Saturday and
Sunday 10:30 A.M. to 4:30 P.M.;
closed Monday

COLORADO

DENVER BOTANIC GARDEN
1005 York Street
Denver, CO 80206
PHONE: 303-370-8010
HOURS: 9:00 A.M. to 5:00 P.M.

CONNECTICUT

ELIZABETH PARK ROSE GARDEN
150 Walbridge Road
West Hartford, CT 06119
PHONE: 860-242-0017
HOURS: dawn to dusk

FLORIDA

FLORIDA CYPRESS GARDENS
2641 South Lake Summit Drive
Cypress Gardens, FL 33884
PHONE: 941-324-2111
HOURS: 9:00 A.M. to 5:30 P.M.

WALT DISNEY WORLD
Box 10000
Lake Buena Vista, FL 32830
PHONE: 407-824-4321
HOURS: 11:00 A.M. to 9:00 P.M.

IDAHO

BOISE PARK SYSTEM
Julia Davis Park Memorial
 Rose Garden
The Boise River and
 Capitol Boulevard
Boise, ID 83706
PHONE: 208-384-4327
HOURS: sunrise to dusk

ILLINOIS

CHICAGO BOTANIC GARDENS
1000 Lake Cook Road
Glencoe, IL 60022
PHONE: 847-835-5440
HOURS: 8:00 A.M. to sunset

KANSAS

E.F.A. REINISCH ROSE GARDEN
4320 West 10th
Topeka, KS 66604
HOURS: 6:00 A.M. to 11:00 P.M.

LOUISIANA

AMERICAN ROSE CENTER
8877 Jefferson-Paige Road
Shreveport, LA 71119
PHONE: 318-938-5402
HOURS: 9:00 A.M. to 5:00 P.M.

MISSOURI

JACOB L. LOOSE MEMORIAL PARK
52nd Street at Pennsylvania Avenue
Kansas City, MO 64112
PHONE: 816-561-9710
HOURS: 6:00 A.M. to 10:00 P.M.

MISSOURI BOTANICAL GARDEN
3444 Shaw Boulevard
St Louis, MO 63110
PHONE: 314-577-5100
HOURS: 9:00 A.M. to 8:00 P.M.

NEW MEXICO

ALBUQUERQUE ROSE GARDEN
8205 Apache NE
Albuquerque, NM 87110
PHONE: 505-296-6020
HOURS: dawn to dusk

NEW YORK

BROOKLYN BOTANIC GARDEN
The Cranford Rose Garden
1000 Washington Avenue
Brooklyn, NY 11225
PHONE: 718-622-4433
HOURS: November through March
weekdays 8:00 A.M. to 4:30 P.M.,
weekends 10:00 A.M. to 4:30 P.M.;
April through October weekdays 8:00
A.M. to 6:00 P.M., weekends 10:00
A.M. to 6:00 P.M.; closed Mondays

THE HOPE ROSARY
Cathedral of St John the Divine
1047 Amsterdam Avenue at
West 112th Street
New York, NY 10025
PHONE: 212-316-7400
HOURS: 7:00 A.M. to dusk

OLD WESTBURY GARDENS
71 Old Westbury Road
Old Westbury, NY 11568
PHONE: 800-651-6955
HOURS: 10:00 A.M. to 5:00 P.M.;
closed Tuesday

NORTH CAROLINA

BILTMORE ESTATE
One North Pack Square
Asheville, NC 28801
PHONE: 800-543-2961
HOURS: 9:00 A.M. to 5:00 P.M.

OREGON

HEIRLOOM OLD GARDEN ROSES
24062 Riverside Drive NE
St Paul, OR 97137
PHONE: 503-538-1576
HOURS: May through August 9:00 A.M.
to 5:00 P.M.; September through April
9:00 A.M. to 4:00 P.M.

**INTERNATIONAL ROSE TEST
GARDEN**
400 Southwest Kingston Avenue
Portland, OR 97201
HOURS: 9:00 A.M. to 5:00 P.M.

PENNSYLVANIA

LONGWOOD GARDENS
Route 1 South
Kennett Square, PA 19348
PHONE: 610-388-1000
HOURS: 9:00 A.M. to 5:00 P.M.

SCOTT ARBORETUM
500 College Avenue
Swarthmore, PA 19081
PHONE: 610-328-8025
HOURS: dawn to dusk

WASHINGTON

BLOSSOMS & BLOOMERS
11415 East Krueger Lane
Spokane, WA 22003
PHONE: 509-922-1344
HOURS: 10:00 A.M. to 4:00 P.M.;
open May and June only

WISCONSIN

BOERNER BOTANICAL GARDENS
5879 South 92nd Street
Hales Corners, WI 53130
PHONE: 414-425-1432
HOURS: 8:00 A.M. to sunset

Appendix C

INDEX *of* ROSES *by* COLOR

This is a complete listing of all the English Roses included in this book. Each cultivar is listed by **COLOR** first (in color-wheel style), then in **ALPHABETICAL** order. A **NOTABLE QUALITY** for each cultivar and the eventual **HEIGHT** are also given.

DARK RED

CARDINAL HUME: *purple, tall*
CHIANTI: *purple, tall*
OTHELLO: *dark red, medium tall*
PROSPERO: *fragrant, short*
THE PRINCE: *purple, short*
THE SQUIRE: *red, short*
TRADESCANT: *crimson-purple, medium tall*
WISE PORTIA: *mauve-red, short*

CRIMSON RED

L. D. BRAITHWAITE: *bright red, medium*
REDCOAT: *bright red, medium tall*
THE KNIGHT: *medium red, short*
WENLOCK: *crimson, medium tall*

LIGHT RED

SIR EDWARD ELGAR: *bright pink-red, short*
THE HERBALIST: *semi-double, short*

DARK PINK

CHARMIAN: *deep pink, tall*
DAPPLE DAWN: *single, medium tall*
GERTRUDE JEKYLL: *very fragrant, tall*
HILDA MURRELL: *ruffled pink, medium*
POTTER & MOORE: *prone to disease, short*
SIR CLOUGH: *semi-double, tall*
THE DARK LADY: *pink-mauve, short*
WILLIAM SHAKESPEARE: *flat flowers, medium tall*

LILAC-PINK

CHARLES RENNIE MACKINTOSH: *fragrant, medium*
CYMBELINE: *gray-pink, medium tall*

MEDIUM PINK

BIBI MAIZOON: *very fragrant, short*
BOW BELLS: *Bourbon-like, medium*
CANTERBURY: *single, medium*
CONSTANCE SPRY: *once-blooming, tall*
HERO: *semi-double, medium*
MARY ROSE: *Damask-like, medium tall*
PRETTY JESSICA: *double, short*
THE COUNTRYMAN: *fragrant, medium tall*
THE REEVE: *warm pink, medium*
WARWICK CASTLE: *ground cover, short*
WIFE OF BATH: *very fragrant, short*

LIGHT PINK

BELLE STORY: *semi-double, medium*
BROTHER CADFAEL: *Cabbage Rose-like, tall*
CHAUCER: *extremely fragrant, short*
CLAIRE ROSE: *very double, medium tall*
COTTAGE ROSE: *Damask-like, short*
EMANUEL: *fragrant, medium*
KATHRYN MORLEY: *ruffled petals, tall*
LILAC ROSE: *gray-pink, short*
LUCETTA: *semi-double, medium tall*
SIR WALTER RALEIGH: *Gallica-like, medium tall*
TREVOR GRIFFITHS: *fragrant, medium*

BLUSH PINK

COUNTRY LIVING: *prone to disease, short*

EMILY: *deeply cupped, medium*

HERITAGE: *semi-double, medium*

HUNTINGTON'S HERO: *semi-double, short*

LORDLY OBERON: *deeply cupped, tall*

PEACH BLOSSOM: *opalescent flowers, tall*

REDOUTÉ: *very pale, medium*

ST. CECILIA: *creamy, medium tall*

ST. SWITHUN: *ruffled petals, medium tall*

SHARIFA ASMA: *fragrant, short*

SHROPSHIRE LASS: *once-blooming, tall*

WHITE

BREDON: *pompon flowers, short*

DOVE: *Tea Rose-like, short*

FAIR BIANCA: *pure white, short*

FRANCINE AUSTIN: *clustered flowers, short*

GLAMIS CASTLE: *cupped, short*

MOONBEAM: *creamy, short*

PROUD TITANIA: *creamy white, tall*

SWAN: *flat flowers, medium tall*

THE NUN: *tulip-like, medium tall*

THE PRIORESS: *semi-double, medium tall*

WINCHESTER CATHEDRAL: *ruffled petals, medium*

BLUSH YELLOW

CHARLOTTE: *deeply cupped, medium*

ENGLISH GARDEN: *flat flowers, short*

JAYNE AUSTIN: *prone to disease, tall*

MARY WEBB: *lemon fragrance, short*

THE PILGRIM: *very thorny, medium tall*

WILD FLOWER: *single, medium*

YELLOW BUTTON: *small pompons, short*

MEDIUM YELLOW

GRAHAM THOMAS: *buttery yellow, tall*

HAPPY CHILD: *bright color, short*

WINDRUSH: *single, medium tall*

YELLOW CHARLES AUSTIN: *cupped flowers, tall*

DARK YELLOW

GOLDEN CELEBRATION: *deeply cupped, medium*

PEGASUS: *fragrant, medium tall*

YELLOW-APRICOT

CHARLES AUSTIN: *cupped flowers, tall*

ELLEN: *fragrant, short*

JAQUENETTA: *single, medium*

LEANDER: *very fragrant, tall*

SWEET JULIET: *prone to disease, medium tall*

TAMORA: *startling color, short*

ORANGE

PAT AUSTIN: *hot color, short*

PINK-APRICOT

ABRAHAM DARBY: *very fragrant, tall*

ADMIRED MIRANDA: *flat flowers, short*

AMBRIDGE ROSE: *cupped, medium*

CRESSIDA: *powerful fragrance, medium tall*

EVELYN: *strongly fragrant, medium tall*

PERDITA: *flat flowers, medium tall*

THE FRIAR: *weak grower, short*

THE YEOMAN: *strong fragrance, short*

TROILUS: *honey fragrance, short*

SALMON PINK

ENGLISH ELEGANCE: *climber, tall*

LILIAN AUSTIN: *bright flowers, short*

THE ALEXANDRA ROSE: *single, medium tall*